Rich with Real Estate Investments

How to Create Cash Flow and Wealth Through Real Estate Investments Business

Table of Contents

Table of Contents..3
Introduction...5
Chapter 1: Flipping Houses...9
Chapter 2: Real Estate Market Analysis.............................67
Chapter 3: Buying houses for flipping 77
Chapter 4: Rental Property Analysis..................................113
Chapter 5: Tricks to Negotiate House Flipping Deals........163
Chapter 6: Secrets of successful rental property investors...171
Conclusion...179

Introduction

There are many different places you can put your money apart from underneath your pillow. You can set your money in bonds, mutual funds, currencies, savings, stocks, commodities, and of course, real estate investments. Each investment option has negative and positive aspects.

In general, real estate investing is the ownership or sale of land or structures for the ultimate reason of making money. Investment can focus on commercial, residential, or industrial real estate properties.

If you have ever considered purchasing real estate investment, then you have perhaps been curious about how to analyze the financial details of an investment property. Beginners in the real estate investing business often ask: How do real estate investors know whether a particular property for sale would generate a good deal or is a rip-off?

The most common reason people give for investing in real estate is that they are looking for financial freedom, but there are others too. Of course, every person will have his or her reasons. But they are typically looking for:

- Cash flow
- Leverage
- Appreciation
- Depreciation
- Tax benefits

The decision to invest in real estate is personal, and it is better that you sit and agree with your family before you move forward.

Chapter 1: Flipping Houses

What is House Flipping?

House flipping is an exciting business. You purchase a cheap home, make it look better than the way you found it, and sell it for a $30, 000 profit. But the truth behind this real estate business is harsh than one might expect.

Flipping a home requires capital, time, and hard work before it can become an attractive investment. If you are thinking about expanding your business acumen to flipping houses for a profit, then you must be adequately prepared. Hopeful, this book will help you learn how to flip a house.

But first, let us answer some questions related to

house flipping.

Does flipping still work in the current market?

In 2012, the house flipping business seemed like the perfect time for a person with extra money and focused on remodeling. During this period, the market was full of homes left vacant from the waves of foreclosures triggered by the housing bubble that erupted a few years earlier. You could purchase a home from a bank, make any appropriate repairs, install new hardwood floors, apply a fresh coat paint and then sell it at the top of the market.

Nowadays, with a stable economy, most house flippers have that extra money in hand. Additionally, they have been monitoring TV shows, just waiting to get the right bargain to begin their flipping career.

However, with the house flipping market back to pre-recession levels, the number of houses coming on the market every month is low. Bidding competition starts the day a property is listed, driving the sales of homes above the asking price in many cases. Buyers ready to pay extra to occupy the home they purchase are having a hard time to find affordable real estate. This means it is hard for investors searching for houses at lower prices.

With a tight inventory without any hopes for single-family home development to fulfill the demand any soon, is there a chance to make money in the house-flipping industry?

Vincent Harris, CEO, and co-founder of Hoozip, a startup company that creates lead management products and productivity for real estate investors, says yes. However, the way you strike these profitable investments is different.

In today's market, the old recession-era practice of purchasing a house at auction for cheap, doing a small rehab and selling it for a profit after 1-2 months is far less likely to work these days. The second quarter of 2018, only 32 percent of home flips around the nation were bought as a distressed sale-according to ATTOM Data Solutions. This is a drop by 6 percent from the same period in 2017 and lower than half the rate in the first quarter of 2010 when the purchases for distressed properties for flipping houses hit 68.2 percent of all purchases.

It is not just a matter of fewer houses going on the market, and the house-flipping industry has changed in the last few years. You're not competing with local experienced flippers, but giant investors and more prominent companies, usually referred to as iBuyers, have popped to the scene.

Nowadays, house flipping has become a much more mainstream struggle, as more and more companies such as Offerpad, Opendoor, and Zillow offer quick, all-cash purchases for homes to flip and sell them for a profit. These companies certainly provide additional options to home sellers, but their presence results in a competitive environment for other investors.

However, this does not stop people from flipping homes. It is only changing the requirements that an investor should have to succeed. Not only are you supposed to identify the right house with an owner who wants to sell, but you require the financial means to get through the actual work and marketing stages before you can receive a payout.

Ted Karagiannis, is a certified real estate broker working for Warburg Realty, he says that the New York City market dropped last year during the early parts of Summer where buyers were interested in properties but did not make offers. Sellers were left waiting, either aiming to reduce the asking price, or taking the property off the market until the time when it picked back up in the season.

Karagiannis goes on to say that if you have to carry the property for 3-6 months, you need to include that into the purchase price.

However, there is a benefit to being a part-time flipper. While more prominent investors need to compete with companies of all sizes to stay ahead, a weekend warrior wanting to make use of his DIY skills to earn a profit doesn't consider a small payout as damaging to his livelihood. In case he makes $20, 000 on a deal, that is great. That

$20,000 could be enough for college tuition for the flipper's child for a whole year.

Some excellent news for those who want to start real estate investing, whether flipping homes or working as a landlord, you don't necessarily need to have the capital to purchase a property with cash. There are lender firms that move with the pace of the market to help borrowers keep up with the competition by lending money.

Whether you finance or use your cash, first-time investors should revisit their expectations before taking any action for the sake of their finances. It is better to commit your mistake with a smaller rehab and a lower loan than bigger.

So, you need to plan your home remodeling project carefully and take into consideration your skill level together with your budget.

Here are a few things you can do to increase your probability of making enough money flipping houses.

- **Invest small and be smart.**

If you still want to flip a house, don't target the former crack den with burst pipes and a hole in the ceiling. You stand an excellent chance to make a profit with a home that doesn't need a lot of work but can sell at a higher price with little fixes here and there. It is also easier to lure a lender when less risk is required, especially if it is your first time into real estate investing.

Your profit won't be high, but you will not make losses or created a money pit. You don't make a lot of profit on every property, but you can complete enough houses.

Once you verify the house doesn't have problems hidden beneath the surface through an inspection, and you have confirmed on the title for liens or other legal matters connected to the property, including smaller cosmetic changes can attract buyers. Make it a little more special than the norm. That can be realized with the right hardware or sink faucets, and things like that can entice people.

It is also essential that you do sufficient research and digs deep on a property before you make an offer. You want to know that the property history, the home, and the neighborhood lead to an excellent investment in the end.

Karagiannis says that in New York City, it is a pro tip to understand the ins and outs of a condo or co-op building's management and charges. So you need to determine whether the building is an excellent condo, or is the apartment similar to a hotel where people come and go after six months to one year. What are the features you are looking at when you are purchasing a real estate? Many newcomers don't know any of that, and they make big mistakes.

- **Invest differently**

Instead of searching for properties on the local multiple listing service, try to identify properties that are not in the market but have owners who are likely to be interested in selling. Part of Hoozip's offering is to allow customers to analyze property data and determine the kind of homes that are worthy of investing. Besides that, there are property records present through local assessor's offices that show property tax information and reveal how long the property has been owned by the same person, though carrying out such searches on your own could be time-consuming.

This can range from high equity in a home to delinquent property taxes or an owner who recently relocated from a state. But since you are working with individual owners who are probably facing financial problems, empathy contributes a significant percentage of succeeding as an investor.

If you can learn to balance the ability to make the seller feel important while at the same time coming off as a professional, you are more likely to succeed. They want to work with someone genuine.

You can also try to buy and hold onto your property for rental income, though you would need to take on the responsibility of landlord-and all the management and maintenance responsibilities that emerge with it.

- **Wait for the economy to tank**

For house flipping, you need a surplus of homes for

sale to snag great deals on properties to flip. The only way to ensure an excess supply of home is when people can no longer afford to live in them. And that translates to an economic downturn. However, the current status remains bright for real estate values and the bigger economy.

How much money do house flippers make?

These days, more and more people are becoming interested in house flipping business as a way of making extra income. Although flipping a house isn't for everyone, it does provide a means of positive returns for those who have the skill and the ability to invest wisely and work smart. Here is a summary of how much you could earn flipping houses?

The amount of money you make flipping a house is determined by the number of homes you can flip, not in finding a single house that will generate a hefty profit. One of the most constant houses flipping tip you will learn is to search for homes where you can make 10-15 percent profit on the sale after paying realtor fees, repairs, title fees, and financing. While these numbers can change depending on the price range that you are dealing with, professional flippers hope to earn around $25, 000 per flip, although they always target more. What they will not do is buy a house that will only generate a profit of $10, 000, which could be eaten up in case of the unexpected repair process.

What is the average earning flippers make?

The average earning house flippers make in the United States is around $29,500. While that is the average money a house flipper can make, still there is room to make more than that. For example, if you are to flip houses in the retail range of $100, 000-$200, 000. You stand a chance to make a 54% profit on investment.

However, note that the amount of money house

flippers earn in the United States differs from one state to another. In Massachusetts, house flippers made a gross profit of $103, 384 per flip in 2013. In the same year, fins in California recorded $99, 999 per flip. As you can see, how much money you can make varies depending on the state.

Lastly, don't forget that these are average earnings, so there is a good chance that you can make more than this or less depending on your experience and talents. As such, you must first understand the probability and failure rate of house flipping before you can start to flip houses.

What is the level of success for house flippers?

In a perfect world, every flipper would make money from house flipping. It would be a secure investment, and every flipper would be costly.

However, there is no perfect world, and you will need to put in more effort to flip a house. For that reason, it is reasonable to fail in house flipping.

In fact, 40% of house flips don't happen. Out of 40%, 12% go for the breakeven price or a loss before all the expenses are included. Once the costs are included, investors could go out of business. The other 28% percent has a gross profit that is lower than 20%. Sometimes, these flippers rarely break even, but on most occasions, they lose money on the deal. Most flippers spend 20-30% of the buy price working on repairs. This means your gross profit should be a minimum of 30% of the buying price. If it is less than that, you risk losing money.

These numbers could be worrying, but if 40% fail, 60% thrive. The 60% have some common features.

First, they have sufficient capital to take on a project of this size. Real estate investment is costly. Even if you find a great deal on a foreclosed house, you will still have to pay for repairs, and workers, and that can slowly add up. So you must be ready with enough money at your disposal once you pay for the house. Besides, you need extra cash on hand just in case you flip the house and fail to sell immediately.

Successful house flippers have set aside time to deal with the project. You must have months set aside to hunt for a home to buy. Then, you need a few weeks to fix it up, schedule checkups, list it, and sell it. If you know you don't have that time, sure you won't succeed flipping houses.

Also, the most successful investors know how to get repairs finished up quickly. Some know how to repair themselves, while others have contacts of professionals to do the repairs. And this removes the big hustle of looking for professionals.

These investors are also up to date about matters dealing with real estate. It is important that you know when the market is at its peak, and when isn't. You also need to examine the property and see its potential. If you don't know anything about the market, chances are that you will buy a lemon that you will be unable to move. You also could purchase a property at the wrong time.

Successful investors have mastered the art of being

patient. Listing a house for sale and waiting for a buyer can be stressful. You want to unload it fast, and if you lack that patience, you could end up with a bad offer. So you need to know when to hold onto the property and when to release it for sale.

In addition, the best flippers don't exaggerate the price of the property. Instead, they put it for sale at an affordable price, making sure that they can make a nice profit. Inflating the price of a property can be a huge mistake that will cost you so much. For example, the property may waste away on the market if you quote an excellent price.

House flipping can be a risky business, but it is worth it if you make money. Take your time to master the best practices and then get in the game. If you are ready, you can cash in on one house after the next.

How much will you need to fix and flip a house?

There's a lot to consider before you dive into the field of house flipping.

- **Rehab and renovations**

Besides the cost of the house, there are other fees associated with the rehab of the house, including the materials, and hiring contractors to complete the work you can't do. New investors to flipping houses will probably prefer to start with single-family homes vs. multi-family homes to reduce the costs for rehab and renovations.

Of course, the average cost of renovation depends on the current state of the house. A home that requires fresh paint and a new appliance will be less expensive than a home that requires a new roof, or a complete gut job.

Home renovations always fall under three categories: moderate, extensive, and cosmetic. Cosmetic or aesthetic repairs are the least expensive to make, but will significantly contribute to the profit you earn when selling the home.

Purchasing a home that requires some cosmetic repairs and TLC can rapidly increase your return on investment. New investors can learn as they move forward by starting with a home that requires some love and expands to homes that need extensive repairs.

But the exciting thing about house flipping is that with the correct tools, time, and resources, you can successfully flip a house regardless of experienced you are. You will learn a lot from trial and error, but that is all part of the fun. The final goal is to make as much for the home as possible without dedicating a lot of money into it. Replacing cabinet hardware, or providing an interior room, a new coat of paint can give the home an upgraded feel and increase the buying price. When it comes to purchasing new equipment, don't forget to consider the cost of delivery and labor to have them installed correctly.

Moderate repairs consist of things like renovating the bathrooms, kitchens and painting the exterior. These things will demand the knowledge and experience of a certified contractor. This means your labor costs will be more than the cosmetic repairs. Properties that need the following maintenance will perhaps be cheaper to buy, but don't forget to factor the time that it will take to finish these renovations and what costs will be conducted during that time.

Homes that may need another bathroom or have severe problems with the roof or the foundation will be tempting to buy because the acquisition price is meager. Think about the time, money, and dedication before investing in a property that needs more repair.

The longer it takes to flip a house, the more you will have to pay in carrying costs, which comprise financing, utilities, and property taxes. As you become experienced, the period between purchase and sale will drop, and so will the costs. Along the way, you discover the tips and tricks to save money and time. However, if you are new to the game, avoid staying long with a property that takes time to renovate and ends up costing you more.

- **Marketing**

Once the fixing is over, the flipping can take the course. Spreading the word that you have a renovated property for sale might not be easy as you may think. While social media, and "For Sale" signs in the yard are great places to start, you may want to consider including specific marketing techniques to the budget. One of the most common approach to spread the word is working with a realtor.

Realtors do a lot of things behind the scenes so that you can get qualified buyers without spending additional time. Of course, you will need to pay them for their services, but it could be vital if you don't have the time, experience, or connection to market your property correctly.

- **Insurance and utilities**

There's the cost of the house, the cost to conduct repairs, and then there are taxes, legal charges, and insurance. It is important to buy property insurance when you invest in a fix and flip. Property insurance is different depending on the location, so you need to determine the average cost in your area and apply it into your budget.

Contractors need lights and water to complete their jobs, so it is important that you get the utilities for the house up and running as soon as possible to eliminate delays. To get a clue of what this will cost you, you can get in touch with the previous owner to breakdown the average monthly utility bills.

- **Doing the math**

Understanding that there are different factors that add to the cost of fixing and flipping a home is one thing, determining how to work your budget around your special situation-that is something else altogether.

Certain investors pay cash for their first properties, but this is not reasonable for everyone. If you plan to finance your investment, there are a few things you need to consider. First, hard money lenders are in the business of lending money to real estate investors. Unlike traditional mortgage companies, hard money lenders loan cash based on the value of the property. This is a better option when you need more money quickly and want a loan that is more flexible than a traditional mortgage.

Once your financing is in order, there are many numbers to crunch. If you have a solid knowledge of your after-repair value (ARV) will assist you in setting a realistic budget to flip a home. This is the last value of the home after you have done all your magic and finished all the upgrades. A great way to understand your ARV is to review the competition. Look for comparable houses in the area that are similar to your property in location, size, and upgrades. Find out how much they have sold for in the last three months, and this will provide you with a great idea of what the price tag at the finish line will look like in your situation.

The ARV is the overall cost of the purchase price

plus the cost of repairs. Once you have determined the selling price of the home, you will budget accordingly, plus your renovation costs.

The ARV can also help you find the best price to bid on a property. The primary rule is to bid up to 70% of the expected sales price. To determine the best price to bid on a fixer-upper, follow the following formula:

Best bid price = (ARV x 70%)-cost of repairs

This means if you get a property that has an ARV $150, 000 and you note that it is going to demand $30, 000 worth of repairs, the highest price you need to be ready to pay for the property is $75, 000. This will create a buffer when it comes to repairs, marketing, and other costs.

Computing your ROI

Well, is flipping houses profitable? Yes, if done correctly. There is a reason why many people find purpose, excitement, and wealth in this particular real estate investing method. Investors are focused on the end goal and return on investment. There are a few different methods to compute your ROI for fix and flip investments:

- **The out-of-pocket method**

This method uses the money you spend out of pocket to fix and flip the property. In case you are financing the home, the down payment, plus the cost of repairs, is what you apply to calculate the out of pocket amount.

- **The cost method**

Another method to compute your ROI is to divide the equity you have in a home by the sum of all costs. This method demands that you include all expenses that come with the acquisition of the property and the rehab.

To successfully flip a house, you have to approximate how much you need going in and how much every step is going to cost you. From making the smartest bid on a property to computing everything from labor costs to utilities, coming out with a well-thought-out budget before you start is important to your success.

How to find a house to flip?

- **Choose a home market**

When thinking about how to find houses to flip, and before you can even begin the process of finding a specific property, you have to choose which home market you want to concentrate. If you are starting, the answer is straightforward: your backyard. Unless you are a professional flipper wishing to expand his/ her business, you always don't need to look further than your market to identify houses to flip that will be simple and profitable for you.

Flipping in your geographic market offers several advantages. First of all, you understand the area. You know the parts of town that are becoming more or less popular, and you have a test of the culture and attractions of the different neighborhoods. This implies that you will have a better idea of the potential value of a home beyond what's on paper.

Secondly, being physically close to the actual project itself will save you time and money. You will be able to visit the property often, whether before buying or during the process of rehab. You will meet with contractors, and probably screen a few contractor teams before you accept a bid.

Meeting face-to-face with a general contractor team is like a job interview; it is the best way to select intangibles that could be lost over the phone. Having to travel long distances to and from a site to perform these tasks can cause a big headache and extra stress.

Being close to the property also means that you will be able to reveal the home once you list it for sale instead of getting a third party. Keep in mind that every third party you involve in your project is an added advantage that will reduce your margins. The more you can do yourself, the better.

A home market is further defined by the type of home. If you have little experience in the flipping business, you may want to concentrate on liquid products on the market. Think of this as your classic three-bedroom, two-bath home, nothing flashy. The high rate of sale and purchase of these properties, both from homeowners and investors, optimizes your exit strategies. These properties will demand less equity than houses on the higher ends of the market so that you will be risking less of your cash.

Finally, concentrate on homes that require moderate repairs. Working on a larger project requires that you have skills, experience, and a trusted contractor team, so until you have completed several flips, don't take on too much.

- **Find the property**

Once you select your target market, there are different deal sources you can, and should, consider getting a house to flip.

Some of the deal sources include:

- Short sale
- Auctions
- Traditional (MLS)
- Seller direct

- REO

It is critical to note that deal sources vary depending on market conditions. For instance, when house prices are low, auctions tend to be the right place to find houses to flip, while seller direct can be lucrative when home prices are high.

- **Search the MLS**

How do you access it? How do you use it? Is it useful to you?

This is a database managed by real estate brokers listing all properties for sale within a given place, along with their features and important statistics.

The MLS is only available to certified realtors and can cost more than $100 a month to access. If you are not a realtor, the correct way to access this information is to align yourself with one, either as a team member, business partner, or just friendly favor. If you are selecting a realtor to help you in your project, ensure they can access the MLS.

Using MLS to identify houses to flip offers certain benefits in purchasing the right property. For one thing, a lot of properties for sale are listed in one place. Besides, the listings will tend to have more information than what is contained in other sources.

A recent study discovered that houses sell faster through the MLS than those sold by owners directly. Homes that are listed on the MLS have an extensive exposure than those not registered.

If you search for properties listed by brokerage, you will see all the features that brokerage is dealing within the area. In general, the presentation of the following listings is more detailed.

Although the MLS can be critical in your hunt for a property purchase, it is only a tool. Spending some time, and using some ingenuity can provide you with significant real estate investment information, without paying a fee.

- **Become a member of a Real Estate Investment Group**

Join real estate LinkedIn groups, investment forums, and local meetups.

Real estate investment groups have become popular

in recent years. There's perhaps one in your area, and it could be worth checking out. They can provide education and networking opportunities that may be important while hunting for a house to flip. Besides this, real estate listings usually appear on the monthly newsletters and websites of these groups.

There are many online forums that can help you buy a property. Sites such as Biggerpockets.com provide extensive information on real estate investment opportunities. There are also different real estate investment groups on LinkedIn and Facebook. Most of these groups offer you access to meetups, where you will have the chance to meet face-to-face with other investors and prospective property sellers.

- **Go for auctions**

Foreclosure auctions are the best opportunities to get discount purchase. But you will need to pay attention to the bidding wars.

If you can pay cash for your property purchase, you could do well by purchasing property at a sheriff's sale, or private auction.

Many foreclosure auction lists are released by the county a few weeks before the sales. Private auctions are also advertised a few weeks early. By analyzing these lists, you have the chance to get a property before the sale date. However, be aware that while you can see the property from the street, you might not inspect it or trespass to acquire the best look.

Purchasing at an active auction has its own risk of being carried away with the bidding. When a bidding war happens, most bidders forget their pre-auction property analysis and quote more than they expected to pay. While bidding against others for a property, set your limit and hold on to it.

Although there is a lot of potential returns, purchasing at an auction property has another risk. Many auctioneers will ask you to put a 10% of the purchase price down at the time of a winning bid. You will also need to settle within 30 days of the auction. If you fail to resolve, you lose your deposit. Therefore, this method of buying is not for those not ready to take a risk in their house flip.

Financing auction purchases can be very tough. Most lenders will ask for an appraisal, or at least a walkthrough of the property before closing, which is always tricky with auctions. You need to be in a position to pay cash, and if you like, finance the property later on.

- **Seller direct**

When home prices increase, and the market is a bit healthy, finding a house to flip can be very hard. Some of the best deals may not even be on the market as the seller hasn't made a choice to sell yet. Seller direct means approaching homeowners at strategic moments when they haven't listed their homes yet-and presenting an offer on off-market homes.

Tools such as PropStream, FindMotivatedSellersNow, and Rebo Gateway compile and curate publicly available data, and develop "propensity to sell" models which help predict the time when a homeowner may be ready to sell his or her property. Once an opportunity is found, these service providers offer you a chance to send targeted mail and marketing collateral directly to prospective sellers. Check out their site for more information.

The most popular seller direct platform is HomeVestors. You will perhaps identify their "We Buy Ugly Houses" marketing slogan from billboards and commercials all around the country.

- **Classifieds**

Unfortunately, the use of daily newspaper to advertise properties for sale has significantly decreased. Although many local papers have classified ads for properties in their print and online versions, it is not seen as the best source for finding an estate to buy.

Searching the newspaper can consume a lot of time. The listings will extend a large geographic area without a means to digitally search for specific characteristics. In this digital age, that seems impossible.

Most of the websites listed above in the MLS section have done the digital search for real estate investment the habit in almost every part of the United States.

- **Use a wholesaler**

Look for a wholesaler to help you complete your first deal. Wholesalers hunt for rehab properties, and put them under contract, before getting a buyer who will implement the house flip. You take the position of the wholesaler in the agreement, paying charges to the wholesaler for acting as the middleman. Ensure that the wholesaler does not add to himself a large profit margin that he doesn't leave you with any profit.

- **Network-network**

Create a network of finders and contacts because their jobs run across distressed home opportunities.

Flipping a house with no cash and credit

Flipping homes with no money is entirely possible,

not only that, but there's a whole community of investors ready and able to offer you the funds you need to process your first deal. That's right, and there are many investors eager to fill your pockets with their money as long as you can prove to them that you deserve it.

If you want to start investing, then using external money will likely be your quickest means to success, but you need to know who to target. Here are the best options for funding your first deal.

There's no place written that it is a must for an investor to fund a deal using their cash. As it turns out, there are different means for financing a deal, none of which will require you to use money from your pocket. It is easy to say that using money from lenders is the gold standard, at least when it comes to matters to do with real estate. If for nothing else, hard money lenders, private lenders, and any house flipping investors with interest to generate money are all more viable ways to hunt for your next deal.

Without further ado, here are options you can try to flip houses with no cash.

- **Private lenders**

Most of the time, private lenders will act as an investor's main source of funding. Private money lenders include banks. Or anyone with some extra money in their pocket, a desire to invest, and propensity to have their "ears bent." More importantly, they are not connected with a government-backed agency such as Freddie Mac. That is a critical point to make. This means private lenders can make their own rules.

With the ability to set their own rules, these lenders will probably come with a higher lending fee. Although the average rate of private money lenders is higher than that of a traditional lender, the investor can get the money after several days, or sometimes hours. This is the most significant benefit of using private money lenders. They are quick at implementation. The slightly higher rate of interest is worth the cost of admission if it means an investor can get funding in as little time as possible. Most investors find that the speed in which they can make an offer is more critical than the interest rate it came with.

On the other hand, traditional banks may take 30-45 days to process a loan, or get a deal to slip through your fingers.

In exchange for funds, most private money lenders request an insurance policy or a promissory note and mortgage on the subject property. Some private lenders even want borrowers to guarantee the loan with their assets, but everything is discussed first.

- **Partner with house flipping investors**

Private money lenders are an excellent method for investors to flip houses with no money, but this is not the only way. Another way to flip a house without any money is to partner with house flipping investors. It is possible that merging with someone that is already flipping properties can be your next best step, and there is no reason they could not provide you with the funding required. That aside, a partner with money is as good as a private lender or hard money lender.

Rather than taking on your next deal alone, consider working together with house flipping investors. As long as the right alliances are established, there is no reason that your partner cannot fund the deal provided you bring value to the table. It is worth to say, however, that if you aren't adding funds to the partnership, you better add value elsewhere. Maybe you know of a deal, or you have the correct contacts. Regardless of what goes on, as a partner, you must be able to carry your weight. At the very least, working with investors that already have money is a great way to start investing.

How to access credit to flip houses?

- **Fix and Flip Loans**

Before you flip a house, you need to find the property. Once you find the property, you are left with thinking out how to find a funding source for your flip.

Not unless you are independently wealthy, you will

need to borrow money to complete the four parts of your house flip:

1. The purchase price of the property. Depending on the lender, you may be asked to contribute 20%-45% of the purchase price as a down payment.
2. The "holding cost" of the house, and other costs of owning the home while renovations are on-going.
3. Materials and labor for renovation.
4. Closing costs and realtor costs to identify a buyer and sell the property.

The first thing you need to be aware while searching for funding for flipping is that acquiring traditional bank loans to help you fix and flip houses aren't the best option.

As a house flipper, you are a real estate investor, and your income can be irregular. Therefore, most banks will avoid giving you a business loan for fixing and flipping properties. And even when a bank is ready to work with you, their investment might not be the best. In general, bank loans are long-term loans-and most flippers buy, rehab, and sell a house with a few months.

- **Fix and Flip Loans**

Before you flip a house, you need to find the property. Once you find the property, you are left with thinking out how to find a funding source for your flip.

Not unless you are independently wealthy, you will need to borrow money to complete the four parts of your house flip:

5. The purchase price of the property. Depending on the lender, you may be asked to contribute 20%-45% of the purchase price as a down payment.

6. The "holding cost" of the house, and other costs of owning the home while renovations are on-going.

7. Materials and labor for renovation.

8. Closing costs and realtor costs to identify a

buyer and sell the property.

The first thing you need to be aware while searching for funding for flipping is that acquiring traditional bank loans to help you fix and flip houses aren't the best option.

As a house flipper, you are a real estate investor, and your income can be irregular. Therefore, most banks will avoid giving you a business loan for fixing and flipping properties. And even when a bank is ready to work with you, their investment might not be the best. In general, bank loans are long-term loans-and most flippers buy, rehab, and sell a house with a few months.

Since it is hard to get bank loans, flippers always search for other means. New flippers in this business can request for loans from their own network of friends and family. Others consider creative ways, such as home equity. Once you have developed an excellent track record as a house flipper, loans from private investors, and bank lines of credit become a great option.

What you need to do before you request a fix and flip loan

Real estate investment is one of those fields where you learn by doing. The more flips you have, the more you will understand what works and doesn't work for you in matters to do with financing.

However, there are a few aspects of flipping that everyone should know before they resort to funding for flipping houses. By understanding these things, it will quicken the process of borrowing and offer lenders assurances that you can handle everything well.

1. First, each flip should have a business plan

Fix and flip lenders primarily lend money to improve homes that are in poor condition. But no one understands the requirements of a property than you do. You will have to provide the lender with information about each house that you are planning to flip.

This is the point where a house flipping business

plan comes into play. No need to write a 50-page report for each house in your portfolio, but you need to create a comprehensive document on each property that includes the following:

- A thorough analysis of the neighborhood where you plan to purchase the property.
- Precise property address
- A plan B just in case the renovation fails to happen as planned.
- A strategy, timeline, and financial projections for the renovations.
- A professional appraiser's current estimation of the property and approximate valuation after renovations.

Looking into each of these points in your flipping business plan will motivate lenders to treat you seriously. It will further allow you to get a big loan to cover all your costs.

2. Make an accurate estimation of renovation costs

Most flippers end up borrowing enough money from their fix and flip lender. Your entire project can fail if you don't have sufficient funds to pay your contractors. The best way to avoid this problem is to come up with an in-depth scope of work before you apply for the loan. Scope of work is a comprehensive outline of all the renovations you will do on the house, the timeline, and the cost.

To build a scope of work, you will need the assistance of a professional appraiser and contractor. Together, these parties will walk through the property, research similar projects, and estimate the cost and timeline. They will quote the price and schedule and account for unknown contingencies.

You need to have a detailed work scope before getting in touch with a lender, or you won't know the amount of money to borrow. The scope of work will also include two other numbers that are critical for fix and flip lenders: after-repair value and loan-to-value.

Funding options to help you flip homes

1. Friend loans

Personal connections will help you raise the money you need to flip a house. Your friends, uncle, cousin could lend you money to complete your project.

Since family members have a personal relationship with you, they will not charge you a big interest.

However, there are a few things you need to remember when borrowing money from your family and friends. First, write down the terms of the loan. Highlight the interest rate and the period it will take to complete it. A written document enforces the security of the loan. Next, follow all IRS laws and apply that to family investments.

The requirements of a fix and flip loan will change depending on the geographic nature of the market. In general, the borrower doesn't make any payment during the period of renovation but clears everything once he or she sells the house.

In case the borrower defaults the house act as

collateral.

2. Line of credit or home equity loan

You can also make use of the equity in your residence. This only happens if you are a homeowner. A home equity loan grants you access to funding for flipping, and you can use the money as needed. Remember that you only pay interest on the money that you use. A loan is a hefty amount, whereas, with a line of credit, you can ask your highest limit.

Equity is the difference between your mortgage balance and market value. To qualify for a home equity loan, you need at least 20% equity in your house, depending on the amount you want to borrow. Also, you must have good credit and sufficient monthly income to manage your mortgage payments and clear the HEL.

3. 401 (K) Financing

This is another excellent option for financing your fix and flip. However, this is not appropriate for someone nearing retirement age. But for first-time flippers, a loan from your 401(k) might be worth it if the rewards supersede the risks.

Most accounts of employers allow them to request a loan of up to 50% of the account balance, or a $50,000, whichever the amount.

4. Personal loans

An unsecured personal loan is a flexible financing product. Similar to personal loans for business, once you take a personal loan, you can use the money for just any purpose, including financing a fix and flip.

To be approved for a personal loan, you need a credit score of above 650. The rates on personal loans can be as low as 5%, and you pay the loan back in installments over a three –seven-year period. The trick is that the loan amounts are small. So, you might need to combine a personal loan with other loan options to support your fix and flip.

Challenges of flipping houses

Every new business experiences pain. You will need to be ready to deal with unexpected problems. Here are some issues that you may experience while flipping houses.

1. Bad weather

No matter where you live, bad weather is going to interfere with your rehabbing schedule. Maybe it is too windy, and the paint you are using is spreading everywhere on the house, or it is raining when you planned to install the new siding. Regardless of what, you need to be ready with plan B.

Plan B means that you create a backup plan just in case the weather is terrible. It might mean that you work inside all day, or begin the exterior work at 7:30 a.m., before the afternoon showers start. This might mean you roll paint instead of spraying. The main idea is to be proactive and always flexible to do something different when plan A fails.

2. Delays

Nothing is more annoying to the average investor than delays on a flipping project. Service providers may be delayed, especially when they are roofing or doing exterior work. Other delays may include materials that don't arrive on time, machines that break in the middle of a job, personal issues, irresponsible workers, and a host of many other factors.

Even when you complete rehabbing the property and have a contract with a buyer, there could be delays in the closing process.

The solution:

- Have flexible back-up plans
- Always choose the best possible people to work for you
- Never depend on a single company or person to do the work

Last but not least, understand that certain delays are inevitable in a large project. Don't allow it to get you down.

3. Unexpected expenses

While doing your remodeling, you may come across things that you need to do that you had not planned for. For example, there could be mold in your shower wall. A leaking pipe in the water heater. Or a broken water pipe. All these add to unexpected expenses. So while creating a budget, you must try to include the costs of unexpected expenses.

4. Cash flow

When growing a business, you must watch out your cash flow, and in the house flipping business, income comes from the houses we sell. If you are not selling as fast as you expected, you need to have sufficient cash to handle all the operating costs like rent, electricity, and so forth.

With so many on-going projects and houses for sale at once, don't take in any profits until houses sell. Be ready to encounter this problem as you grow your home flipping business.

5. Managing email

This may sound like no big hustle, but it can be quite challenging. Email can divert your attention from the tasks at hand when you keep on checking your inbox.

If you have this problem, then you should do one of three things when you receive a new email.

- Reply timely if it is urgent
- Take action if the email requires something other than a usual reply
- Batch it for later if it is not urgent

6. Not enough skills

Professionals such as carpenters, and plumbers, flip houses as a side job. They have the skills and knowledge to find and fix a house. Some of them also have union jobs that offer employment checks all winter long while they work on their side projects.

The actual money in house flipping arises from sweat equity. If you enjoy laying a carpet, can hang drywall, you have the skills to flip a house. On the other hand, if you are not an expert, you will need to pay a professional to renovate and make all repairs. This means the odds of you earning a profit from your investment will be less.

7. Insufficient knowledge

To succeed, you need to select the right property, in the right place, at the right price. For example, in a neighborhood where houses range $100, 000, you don't expect to find homes that cost $60, 000.

You need to have enough knowledge about flipping houses to eliminate the chances of experiencing many obstacles.

8. Being impatient

Professionals use their time and wait for the right property. First-time flippers hurry to purchase the first house that they come across. Then they appoint the first contractor that prepares a bid to address work that they cannot do themselves.

Experts either do the work themselves or depend on a network of reliable contractors.

Novices looking for a realtor to assist them to sell the house. Experts look "for sale by owner" efforts to reduce their costs and optimize profits. Novices want to rush through the process and earn a fortune. Professionals know that purchasing and selling houses requires time and that the profit margins are sometimes thin.

Risk factors in flipping houses

Homebuilders have a fairly manageable process from the foundation. However, flippers don't know the problems that exist in older homes. That aside, experienced house flippers can still predict risks in the house flipping business and how to eliminate them.

Here are some of the risk factors and considerations to help you secure your investment.

1. Market trends

Which direction is the housing market going? Is it balanced or booming? Is it nearing a crash? Find out with national sources and your local real estate agent for updates on the market. Specifically, you want to understand year-over-year trends and the current average delays on the market in your area.

2. Interest rates

This is something that has to be followed closely. It can put some homes out of reach for some buyers.

3. Valuation

This is the most critical part of measuring a potential deal. What is going to be the selling price? On house flipping TV shows, you will see an investor buying a home, fixing it up, then bring in a realtor who determines the value of the house.

However, experienced investors don't do this, instead they make the original offer to buy depending on what they are certain is the selling price.

You can get the opinion of a broker concerning price from a broker with special training and qualifications. Experience has shown that those who do BPOs always sit at a desk and write BPOs and are not in the field much.

The third source of value is an appraisal. Get an appraiser who can conduct an ARV appraisal depending on your plans. When in doubt, search for multiple valuation opinions. If you fail to purchase the property at the correct price, you have little chance of generating money.

4. Investor ability

Some projects won't fit your skillset. Maybe you are comfortable in a suburban environment updating 10-15-year-old houses with floor coverings, baths, and kitchens. This does not mean that you will automatically be good at changing a 50-year-old 2/1 in the city into a two-story 4/3. The knowledge and skills required for the in-town project are much higher.

It is wise to remain within your ability and divert only when you have a mentor to guide your first deal with you.

5. Hidden or unknown repairs

Virtually every house has them. You might open up

a wall to change a shower and find other issues. You might discover after you buy the house that the ceiling is made of asbestos tile, which is an extra expense.

Problems connected to water infiltration can be anywhere. Water is the greatest enemy of a structure. So you should place a 10% contingency on top of each repair budget. If you fail to spend it, that is more profit. But in most cases, you will spend at least some of it.

6. Challenges with contractors

This is the most critical factor in finding out the success of your deal. The best way you can solve this challenge is to apply a robust screening process. You want to ensure that the contractor is a great person with the skills to do the job at hand.

Have a clear contract, covering each item connected to the completion of this task. Make it your commitment, not his. When things start to go wrong, move quickly. Search for the remedies within the contractor agreement. When it becomes clear he is not fixing the situation, end immediately, change the lockbox codes and move on.

A great screening process will eliminate problems in this particular area.

Chapter 2: Real Estate Market Analysis

A real estate market analysis refers to the process of analyzing a specific real estate market depending on historical and current data to identify the best possible investment property to buy in the market.

It is always known as a comparative real estate market analysis because it depends heavily on comparing investment properties with one another or comparing your investment property to other competing properties in the market.

This chapter helps first-time real estate investors to understand the basics of a real estate market analysis by highlighting its significance in real estate investing and the various steps that any real estate investor should take when running a real estate market analysis.

Why is it critical to do a real estate market analysis?

Understanding how much an investment property is worth is a critical aspect of real estate investing. By having knowledge of the value of your investment and understanding your market, you will manage to make smart investment decisions.

Real estate market analysis is vital for those interested in steady cash flow in real estate. Every real estate investor who steps into the world of real estate has one target in mind: to generate money. Typically, not every property in a real estate market will be optimized for investing, so it makes sense to analyze before making any decisions.

CMA allows investors to find out whether a specific piece of property will be a good investment or not. By carrying out a real estate market analysis, investors will know how much rent to charge, and this will make them set a listing price for the property. Depending on the value of the property, you can charge a percentage ranging from 0.8% to

1.1%. If the value of the property is on the cheaper side, the percentage will lean towards 1.1%. If the property's value is $350, 000 or more, the percentage will be close to 0.8%.

Real estate market analysis is crucial because it restricts real estate investors from falling into the commonly made mistakes of either pricing too high and not getting a buyer or pricing too low and missing out on a good return on investment.

Real estate isn't just about renting out homes; many investors buy and sell to make a profit. For that reason, comparative market analysis is required. By determining the value of the property, you can set a listing price for the property.

Long story short, CMA is a crucial step in real estate for knowing the value, settling listing prices, and charging a fair rent.

Overview of a real estate market analysis

A real estate market analysis has different parts,

and each presents critical information to help decide valuation and financial feasibility. The first part explores the location. Examining the area is more than finding the boundaries but instead involves defining the size of the target market likely to create income.

By accurately assessing and defining the target market and its surrounding, investors can identify the competition and the current supply to fulfill the demand in that location.

The next part requires a detailed analysis of the physical and environmental elements that affect the real estate. Physical factors comprise of things such as soil conditions, natural resources, climate, and transport features.

At the start, certain things may not look good to analyze the returns of a real estate investment. However, the community's neighborhood to an exceptional climate can be critical to the community's economy, industry, and desirability. It will be difficult to fully understand the dynamics of the community without appreciating these physical characteristics.

Apart from the physical elements, the market analysis may also need information related to the surrounding physical characteristics. Typically, this involves comprehensive information about the neighborhood's access to public goods and services. The access to and quality of public resources can be critical to commercial real estate growth. As such, real estate developers must consider whether or not a certain parcel of land has enough access to utilities and whether those utilities are capable of fulfilling extra servicing demands of the new development. If not, the developer must persuade the local government to upgrade utility services in the area. Therefore, the presence of sufficient adequate utility services and construction costs must be overlooked because they can determine the feasibility of any real estate project.

How to perform real estate analysis

Here's a clue as to how CMA is carried out, think of what the 'C' stands for.

A comparative market analysis is done by comparing similar properties that were recently sold to the subject property. The analysis compares the features depending on a lot of factors. Since no two properties are the same, there are some modifications made in the investigation.

It is always recommended to get in touch with a professional to carry out real estate analysis. Doing so will save you time and limit the number of mistakes.

You may find it hard to get the relevant data for analyzing a real estate market, and you may not know how to move on with the different steps needed for analyzing the market, or the investment properties. To conduct a real estate market analysis correctly, you will need to consider specific factors. Here are the basic steps to conduct CMA.

1. Identify the location

We can never stop to stress the significance of finding the best location for your investment property. You want to identify a location that is good for buyers because markets are beneficial for buying investment properties. You want to search for an area with high demand. The demand refers to the number of people who want to live in a given area. The more people who want to live in a particular area, the greater the competition is and this makes homes very expensive.

2. Review your investment property

Now that you have selected a location and the type of property, you can begin to analyze. But before you start the comparative market analysis, you need to carry out property analysis. There are specific elements to remember that will impact the value of your property, such as:

- Recent improvements
- Construction age
- Certain amenities like balcony or swimming

pool

- Size of square footage
- Location
- Number of bathrooms, or bedrooms

3. Search for comparable properties

The next step is to identify similar properties to yours. It is good to look at previous listings within a distance of 1-3-mile radius from your real estate properties in the area that has common characteristics to yours.

These "comparable" are commonly referred to as real estate comps, and they are investment properties that share features with your property. To simplify this step, get a rental property calculator which will automatically return real estate comps when you consider an investment property listing.

4. Compare the properties

This is the last step while analyzing the real estate

market. When you choose potential investment properties, you have to compare their prices. Set the cost of the properties in a range between the highest price and minimum price. From the properties you have chosen, choose one home that is worth more than yours based on the amenities and make it the highest price.

Final thoughts

Real estate market analysis can be scary, especially when you do it yourself. But the good news is that it is not a hard task. However, don't fall into the trap of purchasing an investment property before doing a thorough analysis and keep in mind that your goal in real estate investing is to generate money, and not to lose it!

Chapter 3: Buying houses for flipping

Buying from Absentee Owners

Absentee owners are the most searched types of leads for real estate investors and investment companies. But how can you find them? What are the pros and cons of different methods for gathering these real estate lead lists?

What do you do to optimize the lists once you have the data?

Real estate lead lists

There are different types of leads to help drive business for real estate investors, including:

- Real estate agents
- Divorcees
- Cash buyers

- Private lenders
- And many more.

Absentee owners intersect and can allow one to identify these types of leads as well.

Lead lists come in different forms and can be identified in different ways, including:

- Purchasing lead lists in bulk
- Building your list from scratch
- Using software to source highly sought custom lead lists
- Finding competitor's business to gain their databases
- Buying individual leads
- Collaborating and cross-promoting to others' lists

Creating vs Acquiring lead lists

The two most popular methods to generate leads is to:

1. Market and network to build your list
2. Purchasing existing files or access to them

Both have a higher value. Both have a place in most investor's business plans. However, many don't have the budget or experience to grow a list from scratch in sufficient volume to drive their business and financial goals. It might take time. Typically, it requires extensive marketing to attract people to your website or blog and to convert them through opt-ins to participate and remain on your list.

Getting and tapping into existing lists implies plugging right into data that is already present. This is important for those starting or who need to break through plateaus in their businesses.

The advantages of creating your list

1. Unique lists which may not be as competitive as others
2. Can be performed organically
3. Stronger personal relationships with prospects
4. Contacts who are expecting and have

provided permission to market them

5. Not dependent on third party data or services.

The advantages of finding existing lists

1. Filling the regular demand for fresh prospects
2. Ability to narrow databases immediately
3. Ability to drive growth at any time
4. Speed of generating new business
5. Accuracy in getting highly targeted leads
6. Can be more affordable to generate on a per lead basis

Who are absentee owners?

An absentee owner is an individual who owns the property they do not live in.

They always belong to one of these buckets:

- Owners of inherited property
- Second-home or vacation homeowners
- Debt investors who have foreclosed on the property

- Owners who have had to move and leave a vacant property behind
- Out of are real estate investors

These leads can be useful for networking with:

- Cash buyers
- Distressed property owners
- Private lenders and note investors
- Motivated sellers

Absentee owner leads can be applied by real estate wholesalers, house flippers, and rental property investors.

Type of lists

Real estate lead lists exist in diverse formats. Some are designed for direct mail. Others are important for phone marketing and may have phone contacts, addresses, and names. Some may have email addresses while others are sourced based on the data about the property and homeowners.

The more general it is, the cheaper the lead.

However, the more targeted, the more expensive they might be.

Investors can always filter these leads by multiple factors to customize lists. These filters can include:

- Property location
- Amount of equity
- Property types
- Price ranges
- Presence of financial stress
- Number of bedrooms

Methods to market absentee owners

Armed with these real estate lead lists, investors can launch different marketing campaigns to reach prospects using various mediums and continue connecting until they become customers.

These options comprise:

- Email campaigns
- Radio ads

- Door knocking

- Direct mail

- Retargeting ads on Facebook

- Cable TV advertising

- SMS marketing

- Ringless voicemail

- Cold calling

Buying Bank-Owned Homes

Most beginner investors ignore bank-owned homes, also known as real estate owned properties. But those who take time to understand this kind of property know that they are a good source of investment opportunities. These properties always come with lower prices, high yield profit, and less competition. But like any other real estate investment, you can quickly lose money if you don't know what you are doing. Here is a comprehensive look at bank-owned properties.

What is a bank-owned home?

Before we start, it is important to define what REO property is. These are foreclosed houses that failed to sell at an auction and are now owned by lenders such as a creditor or bank. Lenders foreclose properties when borrowers fail to pay loans and try to sell them to recover their money. When no bidders quote the amount of money sought to cover the mortgage, lenders move on to own the property. As a result, real estate properties become bank-owned homes after going through the foreclosure process.

Below are three stages of the REO process

1. **Loan Default:** This happens when the homeowner fails to pay a mortgage for a given period. Usually, after 90 days of missed payments, the lender will send a notice of default and begin the foreclosure process.
2. **Foreclosure:** This is when the property shifts to foreclosure auction. In this stage, the

lender will try to sell the property to the highest bidder. If it is sold, the bank will take some of the money owed on the mortgage.

3. **Real estate owned.** If the home fails to sell in the previous stage, the bank repossesses the house, and it becomes bank-owned. During this stage, lenders remove the occupant and liens on the property and attempt to sell it on their own.

Is purchasing these properties an excellent investment?

Real estate homes are the best for property investors and many reasons. Here are some benefits that make purchasing bank-owned properties for real estate investment an excellent decision.

1. They are listed at discounted prices

Banks and mortgage lenders fail to accumulate wealth by sticking to non-performing properties. They do so by loaning money to borrowers and collecting interest. Most important, banks don't want loans that don't generate returns. For that reason, when repossessing properties, lenders are ready to part ways with them. Here is the first advantage of investing in foreclosed bank-owned homes for real estate investors.

Banks want to liquidate their REO properties instantly to attain the capital they loaned. It is safe to say that banks are like motivated sellers.

In some instances, they are ready to sell these properties at a discount to avoid holding onto them and lose more capital. For a real estate investor who understands how to identify great deals and complete the REO process, this makes bank-owned homes desirable. Thus, if you want to cheap investment properties, search for bank-owned properties for sale.

2. No outstanding taxes and title liens

If you are going to purchase investment properties through traditional real estate transaction, you are likely to be involved with some problems that complicate and delay the sale. One of the main problems buyers always run into is outstanding taxes and title liens that must be corrected before the purchase of a property. On the other hand, the majority of REO bank-owned properties are free of such problems and other outstanding claims. The reason is once a property becomes REO, the lender clears out any liens against it and ensures all taxes are paid. This helps property investors to save a lot of money and close the deal quickly.

3. There are no homeowners to work with

When there's no outstanding title liens and tax, this means that there's no homeowner to discuss with. When purchasing bank owned homes, you won't talk with sellers without a personal connection to their homes, but with a bank which wants to recover its losses. For a real estate investor, this will help save time during negotiations. This also provides you with another advantage: the ability to analyze the property.

When you purchase an investment property at a foreclosure auction, you might not have the choice to thoroughly analyze it before presenting an offer. However, when the property becomes REO, you can proceed to hire an inspector. This is critical to any investor as a home inspection provides a channel to know everything about the home. By inspecting a home, you can know what needs repair, and you can use that as leverage when the time for negotiation comes.

4. There numerous ways to generate money with REO homes

If you are still thinking about how to invest in bank-owned REO properties to make money in real estate, there is more than one method to decide- depending on your personal goals and strategy. One way is to purchase bank-owned properties for rent. This way, you will generate money through monthly rental income that you get from tenants and generate cash flow. This method allows you to earn from real estate appreciation if you hold onto the rental property for the long term.

In case this is not your best real estate investment plan, try to invest in REO property as a fix and flip.

This way, you will purchase the park for a low price, invest in renovations and home improvements that boost its value, and sell it for a higher price. The fix and flip method is a well-known method of investing in real estate, and when done in the right way, it can generate quick returns.

With all these advantages, there's no reason why bank-owned homes cannot be the source for your next real estate investment. But how can you find these properties?

How to find REO properties

The most critical question that you need to ask yourself is how to identify REO bank-owned properties for sale that will bring returns as investment properties. There are several ways for investors like to search for and identify the bank-owned property in the US. This involves:

1. **Getting in touch with lenders directly:** This is the best way to identify bank-owned properties because lenders are ready to

provide you with a list of their available REO properties for sale. This can also allow you to eliminate competition found on public bank-owned homes listings.

2. **REO Listing Agents:** This is simple and reliable for a real estate investor. These agents can identify different options in your area from more than one lender and help direct you on the correct price.

3. **Bank websites:** Some banks have set a whole department to sell real estate homes. Besides that, parts of their sites are dedicated to their listings-whether it's a residential or commercial bank-owned property.

4. **Search MLS:** Many lenders list REO properties on MLS. This means your real estate agent can assist you in identifying REO investment opportunities in your city.

While these are some ways to find bank-owned real estate property for sale, this is not sufficient for a real estate investor. Great investors only invest in homes, which will, for sure, generate a good profit on investment. Therefore, you will need to have an investment tool to quickly find and analyze the possible returns you will get from purchasing bank-owned foreclosed homes.

Financing Bank Owned REO Properties

Those planning to pay cash for their purchases must present a "Proof of Funds Letter" with their offer from the institution where the money is held. Suppose you don't have the funds to buy the REO in cash? Contrary to some misconceptions, real estate investors can apply other methods of financing to purchase bank-owned properties. With the right credit score, you can still find a pre-approval letter from the lender that owns the property. Some banks decide to finance their REO properties. This increases confidence in you as a buyer and provides them with another method to earn money on the transaction.

Also, there's a wide variety of financing choices present for a bank-owned property. The right option depends on your purpose of buying. As said before, there are many reasons why you would prefer to buy bank-owned properties. They can be rehabbed and rented out, fixed and flipped, or even redeveloped. As a result, you need to select the financing choice that suits your investment strategy of choice. Investors can finance bank owned homes using:

- Stated income loans
- Private money mortgages
- Blanket mortgages
- Interest-only loans
- Hard money loans
- Construction loans
- Real estate crowdfunding

Steps to purchase bank-owned properties

1. Search for a lender and secure financing

Regardless of the type of loan you hope to get for financing bank owned homes for sale, it is important to begin the process and find a pre-approval letter early. Therefore, the first step after getting investment properties you are interested in is to speak to the lender about your financing options. This is important because lenders are motivated to sell and get REO homes off of their books. The readier you are with financing, the better. Being pre-qualified by the lender that owns the home increases the buying process. Also, the lender will know that you are financially qualified to purchase the property, making them likely to accept your offer.

2. Find an agent who understands REO homes

Most real estate investors would forego employing an agent when purchasing their investment properties. Although you can do that, having an agent is still advised particularly for starters in real estate investing.

An agent will partner with you and apply his or her experience to direct you through each step of the process of how to buy bank-owned properties. Also, try to look for an agent who frequently works with these types of real estate properties.

These agents understand the ins and outs of negotiating with lenders to find the best possible price, how to compute the cost of necessary repairs, how to operate within the lender's timeline, and how to prepare for the next step.

3. Narrow down your list of possible properties

Once you have a real estate agent by your side, you can begin to refine your list of bank-owned properties. It is important to have a clear strategy of what you want an investment property to contain. Some key characteristics include:

- Number of bathrooms and bedrooms

- Listing price

- Location and quality of the neighborhood

- Important repairs needed and their effect on the price

Most importantly, you need to consider the expected ROI from this property. After all, you are buying as an investment, so it should be able to generate profit.

4. Find an appraisal and an inspection

While banks price REO bank owned homes below market value, this doesn't imply that purchasing them is an automatic bargain. Certain REOs are discounted because of severe damage or undesirable locations. On the flip side, a bank-owned property can be overpriced based on comparable sales in the area.

Therefore, the next step for a real estate investor is to find an appraisal to show the actual value of the property.

It is also vital to get a home inspection before you

purchase bank-owned foreclosed homes for sale. Some of these properties have been without tenants for quite some time. As such, significant problems can arise, which would cost a lot to repair.

To ensure that an REO home is best for you and that no costly issues are overlooked, look for a professional to inspect the house. A home inspection allows investors to understand the needed repairs and renovations before committing to buy.

5. Present your offer to buy

Once you identify the correct bank-owned property, it is time to present your offer. A great agent will assist you in deciding the type of offer that is likely to be accepted, compile the offer, and submit it to the lender. When presenting an offer on an REO home, don't forget the key issues that were uncovered during the home inspection. If appropriate repairs are well-documented, you can use this to bargain for a low offer. Also, the bank will want to know whether you are a serious buyer who can close and who won't waste their time. A real estate investor can demonstrate this by attaching an earnest money deposit check to the offer.

How much can you quote for bank-owned REOs

This is the most important question everyone wants to know. Investors are attracted to REO properties for their excellent discounts. But, some don't get the deal because they don't know how much to offer. No one wants to pay more for a very cheap property. However, lenders will still not take you seriously if present a low offer. You need to make an offer that has an excellent chance of being accepted and generates value to you. Below are quick tips to help you make a lucrative offer:

- **Do your research:** Ensure the offer is comparable to the recent sales of similar homes in the area. In case you realize that the bank has overpriced the REO home, you can quote a lower price and write your reasons in a cover letter.

- **Document everything:** Lenders already have a clue of what they think the property is worth. However, you can justify your offer by attaching documents about the property's status, approximated costs of renovations, and comparable sales.

- **Demonstrate that you are the easiest buyer:** Banks wants to see that your offer is the most reliable and fastest to close. You can prove that by attaching your approval letter to show how secure and low risk your offer is.

- **Include a net sheet:** This breaks down all of the closing costs so that the bank will see how much they will get from the sale you offer.

6. Discuss terms

Despite the myths, a real estate investor can talk with banks, especially if he or she was the one to get in touch with them first. You can discuss the price, who will pay which costs, the permission to inspect the property, and the closing date. Don't forget that negotiating with lenders for bank owned homes is different from negotiating with homeowners. As said, there are no emotions involved here as there would be when working with a homeowner.

On the other hand, banks take longer to reply to an offer than a homeowner. The reason is that different companies or individuals must check an offer before approving. When lenders respond, they will expect you to react immediately to ensure the purchase process moves on. Also, banks are likely to present a counteroffer as they want to show that they attempted to get the best possible price for the property. An experienced agent can be a valuable person during negotiation.

7. Finalize your loan and close the deal

Once you and the lender reach an agreement, you will need to fill out some paperwork and share information to complete your investment and ensure it matches with your offer. Then, it is time to confirm the status of the title.

In general, banks clear the title before they proceed to sell an REO property, but you cannot assume that this is the case. So, get in touch with lenders to see if the title has been cleared or not and get a title company that is ready to run a title search in case you are expected to do so yourself.

Once your loan is ready, it is time to close. Closing on bank-owned properties is similar to any other closing-but there's a little difference. If you fail to close by the predetermined date, the lender may place a penalty fee for each day beyond the deadline. By adhering to the first step of getting pre-qualified for a loan and obtaining financing, you can avoid any delay.

At the time of closing, you and the lender sign the relevant documents to transfer the house into your name and complete your mortgage. Lastly, once you sign everything and transfer the money, you will receive the keys to your new investment property.

A few things to know before you purchase REO

homes

1. **You might have some competition**: If you believe an REO property is the best deal, chances are other investors will too. In case other offers are on the table, work with your agent to know what the bank needs. This will help you create an excellent offer with a good chance of being accepted.

2. **Make sure you are financially okay:** This goes hand in hand with the previous point. If you get an REO property that needs a lot of work, make sure you are financially stable for the results. This means you need to be able to afford to perform repairs and know how much the home is worth after completing renovations.

3. **Banks sell REO properties "As Is":** Banks aren't interested in spending money on a non-performing property. This means, once you purchase bank-owned homes, you will be left with all the repair work. Keep in mind that some of these properties will have significant

problems which will cost a lot to fix. Again, look for a home inspection to determine any substantial issues and estimate repair costs.

4. **Patience is needed:** REOs require stacks of paperwork that have to be reviewed, which means it can take weeks to hear back from the bank once you submit your offer. Additionally, the negotiation step may take longer as your offer is likely to be met with a counteroffer. You need to be patient and request your agent to keep you updated as you wait.

Purchasing a Foreclosed home at house auctions

What should real estate investors know?

If you are planning to purchase foreclosed home at house auctions, it is not as simple as availing yourself to the auction house and bidding.

There are several things that a real estate investor requires to know before visiting house auctions.

This section will address significant questions about foreclosed home at house auctions.

How can you find public auctions?

Most real estate investors have no issues finding investment property listings, but they don't know where to begin looking for house auctions. There are different places to resort to when considering purchasing a foreclosed home at house auctions.

- Check out websites for house auctions

- Search for house auctions in legal newspapers or legal section of your local newspaper

- Speak to mortgage lenders as they have lists of places for purchasing a foreclosed home at house auctions.

- Visit your local courthouse for information related to public auctions

Something that real estate investors should find out

when purchasing a house at auction is the title "Trustee Sale" as many of the house auctions are listed under this name.

What can you do to prepare for buying a property at auction?

A real estate investor should do everything he or she can to be ready to purchase a foreclosed home at house auction. The first thing to do is to research and know what a foreclosure is and why it can be a great real estate investment opportunity. You should also know other methods of buying a foreclosure, in case you want to explore your options beyond house auctions.

Master the laws about buying foreclosed properties at house auctions

This is very critical, especially since the rules on purchasing a house at auction vary from state to state. For instance, a real estate investor should be ready to pay a sum of money for the investment property at house auctions. The amount differs: It could be the total price of the investment property, or it may be a percentage. It can be paid in cash or cashier's checks. Determine whether there is a timeline to spend the rest of the money.

Some states don't reward ownership of the investment property to the real estate investor instantly after building an auction. Your state may demand that a court declares you as the owner of the investment property, which might take months or even more. Ensure that this period doesn't affect any of your investing goals when purchasing a foreclosed home at house auctions.

Determine the requirements of house auctions

Some auctioneers or auction companies have unique needs that a real estate investor should be aware of. Some charge a fee on top of the price of the investment property. Others require real estate investors to have a check send to the auction company before starting. Contact the auctioneer to find out this information before purchasing a foreclosed home at house auctions.

Visit different public auctions before

purchasing a foreclosed home at house auctions

It is an excellent idea for a real estate investor to visit different house auctions before to learn about the process. There are different kinds of people always interested in purchasing a foreclosed home at house auctions, and it's a great idea to have a feel of the type of competition you will be up against. Review them beforehand, and follow as they bid, so you won't be intimidated when you begin to bid at house auctions. You can still try to get in touch with a real estate investor who has experience buying a foreclosed property at house auctions.

Find out where the auction is held

The location for house auctions is different, so ensure you know where the sale will be held. House auctions are sometimes done at the location of the investment property, but not always. Other places include the local courthouse steps or the site of the auction company.

How much can you bid when purchasing a foreclosed home at house auctions

There are different steps a real estate investor should take when choosing how much to offer for a foreclosed investment property.

Investment property analysis

A real estate investor will most likely not be allowed an inspection when purchasing a foreclosed home at house auctions. But, that doesn't mean you cannot drive by to study the exterior status of the foreclosure and its location. Use any information available from the listing to determine the value of the investment property.

Real estate market analysis

Real estate comps will provide you with the best idea of the value of the investment property. Choose a few options that match up in features to the foreclosed home you want to buy. This will provide you with a realistic market value when you purchase foreclosed home at house auctions.

Consider repairs

This step is somehow difficult because the real estate investor cannot do a walkthrough. Once the value is determined from the last two steps, you can work from there. Repairs need to be between 10%-25% of the value of the investment property. When purchasing a foreclosed property at house auctions, you want to pick the worst-case scenario for repairs. Make sure this does not surpass your budget for buying a house at auction.

The guiding rule when purchasing a foreclosed home at house auctions

Why real estate investors love purchasing a foreclosed property at house auctions is that they can avoid paying less than market value for the investment property. So you need to strive to pay 20% less than the real estate market value of the foreclosed property.

Do all these steps to find out what amount you need to consider bidding at an auction.

How does bidding at an auction work

The process for bidding at an auction is

straightforward and doesn't take long. If you adhere to the advice of observing house auctions before becoming a bidder, you will have a great idea. However, for the sake of getting ready, let us break down the process of purchasing a foreclosed home at house auctions:

- Real estate investors will present their cash to the auctioneer.

- The auctioneer will make any relevant announcements, like foreclosure auctions that have been postponed.

- The auction will begin at a minimum of the mortgage owed for the foreclosed home plus a specific amount.

- Real estate investors will start to submit bids for amounts over the value.

- Once a real estate investor wins, he or she is taken to the side to complete forms, and the bidding for other properties continues.

Tips for purchasing a foreclosed home at house auctions

Understand what you are getting into

Buying a foreclosed home at auctions has its share of problems. Real estate investors have to obey house redemption laws. In case the owner wishes to purchase back the investment property in a given period after foreclosure, you are required to sell it back to him or her. Real estate investors purchasing a house at auction may have to remove the current tenants as well.

Don't be late

House auctions often don't last very long, and a real estate investor who shows up 10 minutes late might have missed out on the foreclosed home he/she had his/her eyes on. Some of the first few investment properties sell for less because real estate investors try to fill out price trends during the process of house auctions. You don't want to miss out if you are fortunate to have your investment property auctioned first.

Open your ears

The auctioneer releases an announcement at the start of house auctions, and before each bidding, these announcements are significant. They could result in any liens on the property that a real estate investor can inherit.

An absolute bid

Follow the steps to check how much to bid when purchasing a foreclosed home at house auctions. Once you place a try, it's final, and you can't go back on it. Make sure you don't bid passed your set budget.

Don't be caught in an abiding war

Real estate investors who are purchasing a foreclosed home at house auctions for the first time can get caught up in a bidding dilemma. Avoid this regardless of what is happening around you. You have a set price in mind for the investment property, stick to it.

Purchasing a foreclosed home at house auctions can be rewarding for a real estate investor. Public auctions can be intimidating, but there is no need to avoid them just because you have no idea what house auctions are all about. Be prepared as much as you can before bidding at an auction, and you may find the best way for you to acquire your investment property.

Chapter 4: Rental Property Analysis

Rental properties are the most popular type of real estate properties around the world. The reason for that is rental properties are easier to manage, and the newest investors choose them as the starting point of their careers.

If you want to invest in a rental property, however, how do you ensure that this is the right property to invest in? How can you be sure that this property will generate profit or enough returns to at least cover all its expenses?

This is the point where rental property analysis becomes essential. By definition, rental property analysis is a process of analyzing an investment property to identify its viability for renting out and the profit that it can generate as an income property.

When it comes to investing in rental property, mastering the process of running the numbers is a crucial aspect to your success in generating money and making a great investment.

If you are planning to get one right, this is perhaps the thing you want to ensure you get it right.

When conducting a rental property analysis, there are several things that you need to consider. Some of these things can directly affect the performance of an income property, while others can be used to measure the performance and determine its returns.

Here are important factors used to analyze the rental property.

1. Location

We can't stress anymore, and the site is an essential metric in real estate investing. The location of income property can directly affect its operation, and it will determine the marketing strategy you need as well as the type of tenants that you want to attract to the property. For instance, investing in a rental property in a college town means that you have to target faculty members or students to make the most out of the location.

2. Your rental strategy

Selecting the perfect rental plan for your income property can either make or break your career. Before you begin to rent out your property, it is important that you consider the available options. There are two main rental strategies to apply, and both cannot work on the same property.

- Long-term rental properties
- Short-term rental properties

For you to choose between the two, you need to use rental property analysis tools to determine the most profitable or optimal rental strategy to apply for every property.

3. Type of property

When you first start to learn about real estate, you don't see the different property types that exist in real estate. From apartment buildings, through luxury houses, to townhomes, vacation homes, and condos, every type of real estate property has its benefits and challenges for being used as a rental property.

When conducting a comparative market analysis, the type of property you invest in is very important.

The comparative market analysis should not consider all properties in the area into consideration. But it should only include properties that resemble your property, which consists of the type of property size, age, and other features.

4. Target Tenants

Tenants are the foundation of every rental property. A tenant is a person who resides on your income property and who pays a monthly/weekly/daily rent in exchange for his/her stay. Probably the most attractive features of rental properties are that the tenants who rent the property are the ones paying off your mortgage and all other expenses associated with the capital from their cash.

But there are also different types of tenants, and you will need to personalize your marketing strategies and home design to satisfy the kind of tenants you want to get.

5. Rental income and cash flow

The rental income of an income property is the amount of rent that you get from your tenants on a monthly, weekly or daily basis. While cash flow is the amount of actual return or loss that the property generates.

The cash flow of an income property is the main factor of its profitability. The cash flow can either be negative or positive, depending on the amount of cash you make or lose.

6. Vacancy and occupancy rates

The vacancy rate of a property is the percentage of time every year that the property remains vacant. The occupancy rate, as you may have guessed, is the percentage of time that the property remains occupied.

In an ideal situation, the occupancy rate of a property should be 100%. This will let you generate a profit from the rental income of the park throughout the whole year.

The vacancy rate is usually computed as an expense. Once you finish calculating the profits that you will make from your rental income and subtracting all other costs, you can then proceed to multiply the amount by the vacancy rate to attain the property's cash flow.

7. Cap rate

Cap rate is a metric used to determine the return on investment of an income property based on the current market value.

The formulae for computing the cap rate is as follows:

Cap Rate = (Net Operating Income)/ Current Market Value) x 100

This metric reveals the property's profitability. The value of the cap rate is also expressed as a percentage. It reveals the amount of profit that you will make every year in comparison to the actual price of the property at the point in time. The cap rate metric doesn't factor the method of financing applied, and it will assume that the property is fully purchased with cash.

8. Cash on Cash Return

While the money on cash return is used to determine the profit on the investment of an income property, it is different from the cap rate metric that it factors in the method of financing. More accurately, the cash on cash profit only factors into account the actual money invested in the property's purchase.

Thus, if you buy a property using 80% borrowed cash and 20% cash, the cash on cash return metric will only take 20% cash in its computation.

The standard formula for determining the cash on cash return includes:

Cash on Cash Return = (NOI/Cash Invested) x 100

This cash on cash return is also expressed as a percentage, and it reveals the amount of money that you will earn every year out of the total amount of cash that you have invested in the property.

Analyzing rental property

Whether we admit it or not, when we get started in real estate investing, we will be taking our financial futures into our own hands.

And this can be scary to many people.

But it can also be empowering to most people.

Typically, when people start to invest in rental property, they are worried about making mistakes.

But the fact is that there are many important resources out there that can help you in your endeavor that you need to feel relieved.

And when it comes to analyzing prospective deals, there is no subjectivity.

You don't need to be a genius to see the future or master some numbers.

You only need to be aware of the numbers and tool that can help you compute your return.

So, if you are curious to learn more about rental

property investing, keep reading.

Numbers that you need to know when you run a property analysis

Overall, a property analysis consists of a bunch of different names that relate to property and computing them together to determine the type of return that property will generate for you.

If you are missing any of these numbers, or they are not accurate, it will result in an inaccurate estimation of your ROI.

The truth is that it might take a bit of research to find these numbers. It might require a phone call to a real estate agent or your insurance agent to send you estimates of some of these numbers.

But the research and phone calls are important to attain an accurate estimate of your return.

Let us dive in and find out the kind of numbers you need to consider:

1. List price

This is the price sellers ask for the property

2. Insurance

This is an estimate of the yearly premium for insurance on the property.

3. Taxes

What are the total yearly fees for the property?

4. Utilities

If you are going to pay utilities on the property, you may want to ask the sellers for information on what services have cost them.

5. Capital expenditures

These are costs related to big-ticket items that you will need to replace that cost more money. You might account for saving a percentage or dollar amount every month to go towards your capital expenditure.

6. Condo fees

If the property is located in any association, you may want to calculate the monthly cost.

7. Vacancy rate

The truth of owning property is that it will remain vacant from time to time. You can account the time it costs you money and alters your ROI at the start when you run an analysis. Real estate agents can offer you an estimated percentage of vacancy rate in your area.

8. Monthly rent

You may want to include the monthly rent that you can charge on your property.

If you plan to use financing, you will have to include:

9. Down payment

How much are you going to pay for the property? The loan product you are going to apply may reveal the amount of down payment you will need to pay.

10.   Rate of interest

Interest rates always change in a country. Your credit and loan product may dictate the type of interest rate you earn. Besides, going by the kind of lending institution you attend, it might affect the scale too.

11.   Terms of mortgage

The loan product will define your terms. Essentially, you will see loan terms in increments of 15, 20, 30 years. Typically, for a normal conventional loan, you will be targeting 20% down on a 30-year term.

Entering these numbers into a calculator or property analyzer can automatically compute your ROI and projected monthly cash flow so that you have a reasonable estimate of whether the property accomplishes your investing goals.

Exploring return on investment

If you don't know what return on investment is, don't worry, soon you're going to learn everything.

By definition, return on investment refers to a percentage that is computed by taking into consideration the total net income a property generates and dividing it by the total cash invested.

This percentage reveals an idea of the type of investment return you're making on your total investment.

The most significant advantage of rental property investing is that the return you generate on your investment depends on your market, and your ability to hustle and find a great deal.

When we consider the different avenues, we take to invest the returns that we can probably make have a limit.

For example, in the stock market, the average return is 7%.

With bonds, you can earn less than 5% profit.

And the fact here is that there is no much you can do to make that profit grow.

However, with the rental property, you have the opportunity to invest in assets that generate a return of 12%, 15% or even 20%+

There are properties that make over 20%.

The painful truth

The purpose of investing in rental property is to make money.

This money helps you have the personal freedom to move on with your life.

However, to realize this freedom, you need to ensure that you only buy the right properties that will earn generate money later.

And the only way you can buy the right properties is to do a thorough research of the market. Next, master how to run numbers so that you can find a close estimate of the type of return the property can produce.

Tips for running numbers on a property

When running numbers on rental properties, you need to ensure that you get it right.

We can't stress any more than when investing in rental property, and the numbers should guide you in the decisions you make. It is not an emotional decision.

It is an investment decision. And you need tools to

help you ensure that you are looking at the numbers precisely.

1. Use a property calculator or analyzer

When getting started, you are perhaps wondering ...can I find out all the numbers mentioned earlier...but what can I do with them?

And it's a valid question. Most of us aren't going to sit down and come up with a clear excel spreadsheet that runs the numbers for you.

There are many resources out there that can help you run the numbers on properties. There are free analyzers and free apps that are mortgage calculators that can provide you with an idea of what mortgage would like so that you don't need to figure it out on your own.

The best thing about these calculators is that you need to enter all of the information about the property, and it will compute your return on investment and cash flow.

So that you know immediately whether that property fulfills your return on investment goals.

If it doesn't, then it is easy to say no, and keep looking.

Not only does having a tool like this makes it easier to qualify a property for you, but it saves you a lot of time too.

2. Numbers are black and white

For some, this makes them breathe easily.

For those who prefer a gray area, this could be difficult to handle.

But the reality is that numbers are not subjective.

There is data and information out there that you will find on each and every property that will allow you to perform back and white analysis of a property.

Remember that in the rental property investing, there is some subjectivity in the decisions we make. The location, the type of tenant you appoint in the property and the condition of the property.

Those things don't look black and white.

But when it comes to matters to do with numbers...

it has to be.

When you analyze a property, and it generates your projected ROI and cash flow, you have to trust it.

You get the emotion and concentrate on what the property will make you and whether that accomplishes your profit goals as an investor.

Mistakes to avoid while analyzing rentals

1. Avoid underestimating expenses...if anything overestimates

You'll see once you begin running numbers on deals and researching prospective properties online that you cannot always get accurate figures on the sale.

Any time this happens, we tend to apply our experience quote an estimate. However, one thing that we always do is overestimate.

It is better to be in a situation where the numbers come in lower on the closing day than they are projected.

If you like to underestimate numbers, this can turn to be a great deal. If numbers are tight to start with and you underestimate by even $100 on something, that could make a once seemingly profitable property a bust.

2. Don't believe everything that the seller says

When you are getting started, it is easy to trust anything that someone tells you.

But that is not right; you need to toughen up a bit and think a little before you do anything.

You must try to verify whatever people say to determine whether it is right or wrong.

Keep in mind that you have the right to request for verification of numbers that they are giving you, don't feel like you are too pushy.

What you are doing is protecting yourself and your money.

How to determine the sales price of a property

There's no secure method to determine the exact value of your current property or the property you want to buy.

Becoming wealthy in real estate involves purchasing, maintaining, and holding for as long as possible to build wealth.

Fundamentals of valuing property

1. It's all about income.

In real estate investing, you need to have a precise target of income that you want a property to generate every year. Both the past and current figure's what is essential.

Once you come up with a range of income, you can move on to calculate the gross rental production of the property and compare with neighborhood properties.

2. Appreciation of price is secondary

The primary reason why there has been a housing bubble, and later, a collapse is because investors migrated from the income aspect of the property and concentrated on prospective property appreciation.

Investors don't care that they were substantial negative cash flow if they drive the wave and flip for profits with 1-2 years.

3. Property is always local

Be keen that you don't overestimate the property statistics. The correct means to determine the value of your home is to factor in the price which your neighbor sells. Property statics demonstrates the general direction of costs and the relative strength.

Estimating Rehab Costs for Real Estate Investors

Estimating the costs of rehab can be the most challenging and important elements to successful property investing. When you approximate a fix and flip renovation project too low, you will lose out on your profit. If you quote a higher estimate, another investor will grab the deal.

Well, how can you estimate home repair costs when you don't have a construction background? How can you compute rehab projects to make sure you will earn profit you want as a property investor?

First, let us find out why accurate estimations of repair costs are important.

One of the most common mistakes that new investors make is inaccurately quoting structural repair costs such as re-plumbs, re-roofs, and heating and cooling system replacements plus cosmetic improvements like new flooring, paint, and fixtures.

You will be surprised by how new buyers get it wrong when they are assessing a property. Typically, they overestimate the costs related to fixing up the home. Some may do it out of ignorance, but those who know better do it as a way to justify making a low-ball offer on a property. On the flip side, underestimating costs can be dangerous. Either way, you are preparing for investment failure.

Here is the reason: If you underestimate the costs of rehabbing a house, you will spend a lot of time rehabbing it, but you will realize when you resell it that your profit will be far less than you expected. That may seriously discourage you from ever wanting to take on another flipping project and damage what could be a promising means to create wealth.

Similarly, if you overestimate the cost of a project, you may either quote a low bid to be accepted by the seller or be beaten out of the deal by another investor who approximated costs correctly and was able to outbid you. You could even choose to pass on a property that would have earned you a huge profit. Good deals take time to find; thus, a lost opportunity can be expensive.

Simple steps to estimate the rehab costs

1. Know your buyer and the neighborhood

Before you begin to calculate the amount of cash it will cost you to rehab the property, you must understand how the end product will look like. There are advanced models that take months, and there are quick flips that take only days. Knowing the level of finishing to which your buyers want to rehab the property is important. Besides, looking at the property around the neighborhood will provide you a good knowledge of how far the rehab may be required. In general, investors don't want to go too far and beyond the practical level of other properties around the neighborhood. For that reason, if the house is in a working-class neighborhood with many working-class rentals, you don't need to spend hundreds of thousands on a rehab.

2. Visit the property

Once you have enough information on how the end product should be, next is to visit the property. You can take pictures, or record video with your phone to help you remember how the feature appears. Photos will help you sell the property to the cash buyer. So, you need to let the seller know that you will be taking pictures for analysis and that you won't release the photos to the public.

3. List the problems you find in every part of the property

While you are at the property, walk-in every room and note down the condition. If a specific part requires replacement, write it down. For instance, if you see a torn carpet in the living room, you need to write it down. You should not forget to write down a quick approximation of the room, make your guess. Be sure to look at the exterior section of the home, and see whether there are any issues.

Tips to get accurate estimates for house flips

House flipping is something that every real estate investor has tried to do at one point or another. It provides a chance for high returns over a short period, but it can also be costly if you don't know what you are doing when flipping a house.

Besides choosing the right property, one of the most critical skills is to accurately estimate repair costs on the front end, so you optimize profits on the back end. Although this is an acquired skill that you will become better with time, you must learn about how to estimate the costs of rehab before starting your first deal.

Check out these tips to help you make accurate estimates for a house flip

There is no perfect method for estimating repair costs. However, there are a few rules and techniques that you can apply to get accurate estimates.

- **Identify the things that need to be fixed**

It is hard to estimate repair and rehab costs if you don't know what needs to be repaired or fixed. Before you look for a professional, you must take an inventory of the home's condition and evaluate the problem areas.

When you invest in a house, you want something with good bones. Think twice about investing in a home that has issues with the roof, structure, and foundation. Other expensive stuff includes plumbing, HVAC, and electrical.

Typically, a house flip requires cosmetic work. Things such as countertops, appliances, landscaping are all cost-effective fixes.

- **Develop a ballpark estimate**

Although the price per square foot rule of thumb is suitable for a nice round number, you may want to develop a more accurate estimate if you are considering purchasing a flip house.

To avoid overestimating, it is better to itemize each repair and develop an average cost.

First, compute the total list of materials required, and record both high and low estimate for each. Once that's done, include both columns of numbers to get the total cost for both top and small real estate investors.

You will also need to know the labor costs and what contractors charge for their time. When you begin to build relationships with contractors and offer them lots of work, you will discover that their rates reduce.

- **Determine the carrying costs**

Apart from calculating the rehab costs, prepare for carrying costs. These are the costs that you are charged during a repair. If you are financing the deal, it includes payments and interest. If you pay in cash, you will still incur property taxes and other expenses. Consider this because they affect your budget.

- **Search for hidden costs**

In a house flip, it is not the repairs you know that you need to be worried about. Instead, the hidden costs that you haven't factored for that will do you in.

For newbies, hire a professional inspector, or contractor to do the work. This will save you from the other costs that you didn't expect. These professional inspections, along with structural control, can cost you around $200. Which is nothing compared to the value of the damage that might be lurking in the foundation or even in the roof if you are not careful?

Another thing is that you need to expect costs to differ. Some of your estimates will be low because of unexpected repairs that you didn't consider, while other large costs you estimated may prove to be less than your original estimates.

I remember a time when I thought an air conditioning unit might require replacing for $2,000-$3,000, only to happily realize that a simple $200 repair made it work like new. Also, by shopping carefully across different stores, using credit cards that have discount and buying items when they're on sale, I tend to find materials that reduce the costs below the original numbers.

Here's a quick tip. Since the more time you spend before you re-sale the property, the higher your expenses such as utilities, taxes, maintenance, and insurance become, the faster you complete the re-sale, the more significant profit you earn. There is a time I spent $500 on custom cabinet doors before closing because I wanted to attain a head start on rehabbing, only to discover a week before we closed that title problems were going to prevent us from closing at all. That was money lost.

- **Build a checklist of items before visiting a property**

One way that you can ensure that you don't miss any cost is to develop a list of items.

There are different kinds of the checklist, so you need to look for one that is fit for property investing and rehab projects. While every property may have its unique features, and requirements, it is good to have a basic template to guide you on the main areas of any repair.

- **If you are not confident enough with a checklist, hire a contractor**

If you doubt a list, then proceed to look for an experienced contractor to inspect the property with you. Allow him to set the bid price for the project and use that bid as an estimate for rehab expenses.

- **Compute your estimate based on square footage**

Don't be concerned with the details of every room.

Make an estimate based on the total square footage and break down the individual rooms that require more work.

- **For major mechanicals like electrical and air conditioning, apply your confidence to create the estimate.**

This means if you believe 25% of plumbing may need repair, you need to include that in your rehab costs.

This will ensure that adequately plan your money to perform repairs. However, if you don't need to make these repairs, you will be okay. Keep in mind that as you continue to invest in more properties, the cost will even out.

This is the best way to be sure that you take into consideration "potential, "larger expenses. But in case you forget to estimate rehab costs in "potential" costs, you might lose money.

Lastly, remember that you can spend more on a home that you are going to flip than rent because you will earn the profit on your dollars quickly on a flip.

These tips will help you to win more offers and boost your profits on all your real estate investments.

Finding the best rehab real estate for sale

Rather than searching and discussing deals with different realtors and homeowners, most rehabbers resort to property wholesalers to provide them with the best deals.

Why?

It is easy and effective. Also, wholesalers are more convenient.

They have a broad experience in getting the best deals. They handle all the marketing and contracting tasks, so you stick to rehab and flipping the property to earn a profit.

Repair most investors avoid –but should not

Foundation work

Most property investors and homebuyers look at home foundation problems and walk away. But it provides a great opportunity. You can get a great deal on the property as others avoid it.

To confidently estimate the foundation work, get a structural engineer to report on what action the foundation requires. Take the report to a foundation repair company and request them for an estimate for the work quoted in the story.

Involving a foundation repair company often leads to a high estimate because they have the incentive to give you an estimate for all the possible work, and perhaps even more, than the foundation may demand at this time.

A quick tip: When approximating the cost of rehab, don't forget to ask whether the interior flooring will be destroyed during the foundation work. If so, make sure you include this cost in your rehab estimate.

Getting a rehab loan

You should be prepared to make an offer when a great opportunity arises by qualifying to earn hard money loan.

For home rehab projects, hard money or cash could be your financing choice because conventional lenders cannot take the risk on a property that is in poor condition.

Besides, traditional loans take more time. But hard money loans are meant to be fast and easy, and that is why you should not miss any investment opportunity that presents itself.

If you choose to use real money, you may later regret. It is very risky, especially when you run out of cash.

But with hard money loans, you still get leverage to complete multiple deals. In real estate investing, the more deals you make, the better it will be for your bottom line.

Search for a hard money lender whose team comprises of investors themselves. This offers them the correct expertise and the desire to teach you on the exact steps and opportunities to take for your rehab projects.

The advice you get from hard money lenders is critical and can be the difference between success and failure. You may miss this mentorship if you decide to use your own money to fund everything. Remember, conventional lenders, don't have the experience and skills to offer you tips on rehabbing costs plus other areas.

How to realistically budget for rehab costs

Whether you have watched many house-flipping TV shows or have recently decided to invest in rental properties, there's more that you need to learn before choosing the perfect home to rehab and resell.

When it comes to house flipping, many newbies make the mistake of underestimating the overall cost of repairs and finally lose money because they forgot to include certain expenses. To record a profit from a fix-and-flips, you need to have good knowledge of the fix-and-flip process, which involves the acquisition of property, budgeting the repair costs, the fix and flip process, and lastly, the sale and marketing of the property on the back end.

The secret to making money from flipping houses is to precisely predict the amount of money you will spend on each property. This will help you estimate the profit on the projected selling price. But, getting the budget right isn't easy, mainly when you are new to the business.

Here's how you can build an accurate budget for fix and flip renovations.

Just like gambling, don't invest more than you can afford to lose when flipping homes. Before you start pricing houses, set a rehab budget, and analyzing buying and selling costs, determine the amount of money, you can afford to lose in a worst-case scenario. Once you agree on that figure, you can better plan how many houses to buy and how much to flip it.

Set the maximum amount of money you want to risk on your flip. This may comprise of a loss you are ready to take in case you have to sell the house quickly, or extra monthly debt payments you can control if you end up failing to sell the house.

Organize the budget into four sections: selling costs, house purchase, upgrades, and carrying costs. Now calculate how much cash and credit you will need to do the flip.

Get in touch with a real estate agent to evaluate the purchase price of your house vs. your budget. The more properties you buy, the less money you will need to upgrade it and vice versa. Request the agent to recommend to your houses you can purchase and rehab that meets your budget and the expected sale price and profit will be if you fulfill your projections. For every property, ask for a comp report, which reveals the prices for which comparable homes in the area have sold.

Determine the buying, selling, and carrying costs for different house prices in your initial budget. Add the down payment, closing costs, real estate agent commissions, sale of the house, and any other inspection fees, interest, and taxes. Budget for a complete inspection to cut down the chances of purchasing a home with issues that you might learn only after start your rehab work.

Write down the target budget ratio of a home purchase to rehab costs. However, if you can buy a property for a little money, you can include more of your budget to the rehab. Set aside 15-20 percent of your rehabbing funds to handle unexpected expenses.

Make use of the money you have budgeted to help your real estate agent to choose a house. Tell the agent your profit goal for the flip. An experienced agent will only offer a home that you might buy for a price that leaves you with sufficient money to improve it and sell it at a similar amount for the neighborhood.

Take time to look at houses recommended by the agent, pricing upgrades the agent suggests that you will need to do to calculate your selling price and profit. Get in touch with contractors to determine the exact cost on all construction work like electrical, plumbing, painting, tile, and roofing. Price cabinets, flooring, toilets, and sinks, or any other items you will require if you are doing all or part of the rehab task.

Create budget forms for different home prices. List the buying price on a separate document, including inspections, commissions, and closing costs. Add your budget is remaining for rehab costs. Set your 15-20 percent rehab cushion fee as an expense. Key in your selling and closing costs. Analyze your total costs to check whether they match your available cash or credit line for the project.

Buy a home that leaves you enough money to finish upgrades that will give you a chance to sell it for a price and in a time frame that earns you your desired profit. Consider a realistic selling price and timeline on your agent's assessment of what upgrades should be made to come up with a comparable selling price for the neighborhood.

A quick tip while creating your budget

Try to get as many items as you can to a price per square foot. This will save you time while walking inside the house. The narrow, focused approach will allow you to see little things that you could miss, such as doorknobs, switches, and door stops. Paying attention to the small details will also allow you to determine what you might be able to keep as is, and what can be reused with little repairs, and what will need to be completely repaired.

Once you have your budget ready, it will be easy to make an offer on the property quickly. It is always good to understand your exit strategy before you visit the house. Suppose something happens and you fail to start the rehab project as planned? Will you manage to wholesale the property to a different real estate investor? Suppose you have a problem selling the house after the rehab work is done?

Will you manage to rent the property until you get it sold? Having a plan B in mind will make your whole rehab project less stressful.

How to find the best house flipping contractors?

A right contractor is one who can change the condition of your house so that it is ready to sell.

Unfortunately, there are scary stories of house flipping contractors who have caused a lot of headaches to homeowners.

Fortunately, this section will help you understand how to identify the best contractors to make sure your house flipping business runs smoothly.

First, where can you get the best contractor? Here are some great places that you can check out.

REIC Referrals

For this one, you should start at your trusty local REIC. Investors who attend these meetings will likely have certain referrals for you to pursue. And because you can bet they have worked with them before, you know that the contractors will have an excellent track record. These sorts of network can be essential.

Hardware Stores

You can still find contractors at your local Home Depot or similar hardware store. It is good to show up early so that you know you are working with someone with a great work ethic. You can always identify them because they are the ones purchasing a significant amount of house-rehabbing supplies.

Farm area

Another technique is to drive around your "farm area" and search for contractors working around. It provides you an opportunity to see how they run their projects and the type of work they do in a real-life situation.

Search online

Sometimes, an online search for local contractors can deliver great results. When you find them, ask them for references which you can contact and request to see the projects they have completed. Keep in mind that just because you are calling them, doesn't mean you have to hire them.

The rule of 3

If this is your first time, the Rule of 3 is a powerful tool to help you anytime you want to hire a contractor or service person.

When you start with contractors, focus on getting three different contractors to offer you bids. By the time you meet with all of them and know their perspectives, you will be surprised at how much you have learned.

How to find and work with contractors

House flipping is a team effort. The vital part of most house flipping teams are general contractors, or trained home remodeling professionals who conduct and look at residential rehabilitations and renovations.

A general contractor abbreviated as GC is responsible for providing all the material, equipment, labor, and services required for the project construction.

Do you need a general contractor?

Whether or not you need a general contractor for your property renovations is the first thing to think about. The rule of thumb is that if the project is beyond the basics, then you likely will.

A cosmetic project is one that does not require working on the foundation or critical parts of the property. If your house renovation project is limited to bathroom renovations, kitchen renovations, flooring, paint, and landscaping, you can complete the project yourself or with sub-contractors. Sub-contractors have specialized in specific tasks. Examples of subcontractors include electricians, plumbers, and roofers.

But in case your project is more extensive, and you are working on sections of the home that are key to the home's architecture, you will need a certified general contractor.

It is essential to underline that a general contractor is not only advised but required to complete extensive rehab projects. Different states require a licensed contractor to find the relevant permits from the municipal building department for the project to start.

Also, most lenders will require that the borrower must work with a certified contractor to be lent money per the project's scope of work. State and lender policies will differ, so it is better to carry out your research.

How can you find a general contractor team?

Once you decide you want a general contractor for your house renovations, it is time to look for the right on to partner with. There are many creative ways to identify and screen GCs.

The more confident style to find a reliable team to work with is using referrals. Ask colleagues in the industry which contractors they have worked with and have reputations they can guarantee. Real estate investment clubs in your area will also have official directories of recommended contractors. Search for proven track records of completed projects on time and budget.

Looking at a finished product will present you the

best knowledge of the kind of skills a GC brings to the table, so look out properties they have worked on if you can.

Another way is to search the job sites of houses under construction in the neighborhood. When a contractor team is present and working, flag down a worker, and introduce yourself. Request for contact information or leave your information and request someone to contact you about potential work. Otherwise, there will likely be a sign with their company's name, so you can write it down and search them online.

You can still go to the city's local building department and find out which contractors have been awarded permits for construction. Contractors are asked to file for and obtain permits to do certain work, and the projects must pass an inspection to make sure they are up to the city's code. These permits and inspection are public records, which the building department can offer you.

Real estate is still a bit of an old-fashioned industry, and many house flippers use offline methods such as the ones discussed above. But there are online tools to general source contractors: Online real estate investment communities and connected investors can match flippers with GCs and vice versa, so look out those. You can still try places such as Yelp, Angie's List. Google and see what you will find.

How can you select a team that is perfect for you?

Once you narrow it down to several rehab contractors you want and have collected bids, it's the time to choose which general contractor is best for you.

The first thing to confirm is whether your general contractor is certified in your state. Requirements for licensing differ, but almost all will need a certain number of years of experience and a written test.

You may want to ensure that the GC is specialized in the right fields for your project. To be licensed, a general contractor will require different individual specialties such as concrete plumbing, electric, carpentry, etc.

Being overqualified is not a good thing, so your contractor has a lot of specialties than your project requires, no problem.

Next, ensure that your GCs are insured for an amount more prominent than the risk you are taking on with the project. Every contractor license is bonded with an insurance policy which defines how big of a project the contractor can take on. It is impossible to handle a $1-million-dollar project if your contractor is only insured up to $200, 000. Insurance policies are essential for projects that require municipal infrastructures, such as power lines, and sewer lines.

Beyond the following necessary qualifications, you may want to attain a sense of GCs organizational skills, general professionalism, and communication skills. Can they provide licensing paperwork in a timely way? Can they show pictures and details of their past projects? When collecting bids, pay attention to which teams can price a project accurately, quote a realistic timeline, and foresee potential problems. Stay away from teams that are over comprising or setting aggressive deadlines. Don't forget that flipping a house rarely goes exactly as expected, and yourself space both in terms of time and budget is important.

Trust is also a significant factor in creating a productive working relationship with a contractor. We advise writing shared incentives into contracts that show both parties are dedicated to a successful project.

For instance, suggest penalties in case a project is over budget, and bonuses if the project is early on time. When a contractor quotes 60 days to completion, suggest that completing in over 70 days will result in a penalty, and finishing in under 60 days will earn a bonus.

Or, suggest that they divide the costs of going over the timeline with you to learn how focused they are to sticking to it. There are various material costs to holding onto a property for longer than planned, so if a contractor is ready to commit to a date, they should be willing to commit to helping pay these costs if they miss it.

Be clear on payment expectations. Divide the job into incremental payments, get a signed a contract, and don't ever pay money upfront without a signed contract and payment schedule agreement. In case a contractor stressed on upfront payments without a work schedule, and payment plan, that is a red flag. Work with persons who know how to deal with their finances and don't live from a deal to sell.

Once you have selected a contractor that looks reasonable, trustworthy, professional and charges a price within your budget, you are ready to go.

How can you best work with general contractors?

Once the project is started, it is time to control your team. Like most working relationships, a great mix of autonomy and accountability is the best method.

Set upon a macro level, the kind of projects you need to get done and in what order. For example, you can plan to do foundation, then carpentry, paint, and finally landscaping. Agree on weekly or bi-weekly timelines, but daily, allow contractors to manage themselves. Allow the team to prioritize tasks and control their days, and don't be a micromanager. Keep in mind; they know what they are doing.

To hold them accountable to their deadlines, organize walkthroughs to ensure things progress on the agreed-upon timelines. During these walkthroughs, take note of the teams that are on track per your deadlines and which ones appear to lag. If you see something, say something.

If you are remote, don't be afraid to make the surprise Skype call or FaceTime to get a sense of how things are moving. In case a contractor is not ready to pick up a video call and show you around the property, that is not a good sign. Communication is key.

The correct contractor can and will make a difference in your project. Hope you find these tips helpful and will put them to use.

Chapter 5: Tricks to Negotiate House Flipping Deals

If you are about to finalize a deal on the tremendous asset, you will buy. You must have excellent negotiation skills. Submitting the offer is only the beginning of the negotiation process. There is no secret that the best way to "make" money is negotiating. Check out these tips before making your offer on a home.

1. Look for a professional real estate agent

This is the first thing that you must do. Find a licensed real estate agent. A real estate agent should be an individual you can trust to represent you. This way, you will receive sound advice from a person who has sufficient knowledge in this industry. Learn to ask your real estate agent for help and take advantage of what they know that you may not. Apart from this, don't attempt to speak directly to the seller if you think you may not have enough information about purchasing homes.

2. Do your detailed research

You may have to gather enough information as you can. Do not say that you know everything. Keep asking questions about the property and the seller. Data is a significant tool. The more information you have, the more you can support your argument during a negotiation.

It is better to allow your real estate agent to talk to the seller's broker instead of you. Sometimes, they may not show information to you, but they can to someone working in the same business field.

It is important you understand the type of market you are working in. Is it a buyer's market or seller's market? If it is a buyer's market, and the supply is higher than the demand, the chances for getting a better deal are in your favor. However, if it's a seller's market, it is the opposite, so you must know when selecting a property and submitting the offer. These extra bits of information create a big difference.

Allow your agent to carry out comparative market analysis and identify the relative of your property. This will allow you to know buyers willing to pay for the property, and the way the property compares with other features in the market. By mastering this, you can place the best offer on the property and ensure it compares well in the market.

Before you submit an offer, you must find out a payment scheme if the seller accepts your offer. You don't want to bargain and then experience payment issues. This will also help you make up your mind if you are stuck between choices.

3. Time is critical

Time is a critical aspect, especially in real estate negotiation. Depending on the research, the first opening minutes of negotiation can determine the result. Also, you must learn to be patient. In general, the seller will attempt to close the deal soon as they can. So, try the best you can to extend the time. Don't rush things while negotiating. Keep your offers running and try to counter the seller's offer.

But keep in mind that this is not going to be easy. Therefore, you need to master how to extend the negotiation process; you could miss your opportunity because of attempting to have the last concession.

When you alter time, you can benefit from creating a sense of urgency. Use time as a tool to force the seller into accepting the offer. Additionally, if your offer is lower than what another buyer has quoted, you can use the time to finalize your payment.

4. Master the art of communicating well

This is the most vital skill in any negotiation. You must ensure that the seller knows where you stand. Let him, or she know your stand by submitting your offer, expected closing date, and the methods which you are going to make payment.

An important communication tool is to understand what to speak when to speak and how to speak. Sometimes, being silent is the best thing you can do. Practice listening more than you talk.

When saying your price, say it with confidence. Say

how it is going to benefit yourself and the seller. However, don't justify the offer using any means or present inappropriate information.

We cannot stress this anymore; try to be in touch with a real estate agent. These are people with many years of experience and understand the way to speak to a seller or real estate agent.

5. Remain positive and confident

Even when things aren't going as planned, do not lose control. Maintain a healthy and positive attitude. Don't begin to think of where your best sofa set would go. Emotions can interfere with your judgment. Spend some time to analyze your choices pragmatically. Consider it as a business deal. In case it fails, you will close another one. This is why we stress that you consider various options and maintain an open mind when choosing property.

6. Review your finances

Before you present any offer, you must know how much you want to finance your investment property. This will allow you to negotiate well, and understand the amount of money you can invest, and the returns you will generate when you buy an investment property. It will further provide you a clue of how much you can negotiate with the seller.

Create an exciting offer, but still leave room to increase it. This will make sure that you maintain a firm stand when negotiating, and will provide you the flexibility.

You must ensure you have enough money to buy an investment property. If you are getting started in real estate investing, it can be hard, but there are many ways to save money so that you make more in real estate.

7. Don't hang up on small things

Some things don't warranty getting hung upon. Don't miss out on a prominent real estate investment deal because you are bargaining several thousand dollars, or thinking the property décor is not good. If you have chosen your finances, you need to have a great idea of the interest you want to pay, and you can figure out how much you can change and adjust well.

Another tip is that you must leave your ego aside. This may look like a no-brainer, but some real estate investment risk losing a whole deal simply because they want a concession. So, avoid putting yourself in that position when you are about to purchase an investment property. Unless the property you are buying is your own, don't be caught up in small things.

All in all

Real estate negotiation, when purchasing an investment property, can be hard and frustrating. Even so, keep in mind that both you and the seller want to get the most out of the deal. The seller is not your enemy, nor is he/she working against you. So, try to work together during the negotiation period to reach an agreement that you are both okay with.

Chapter 6: Secrets of successful rental property investors

Do you know why some real estate investors make millions while others fail?

The secret could be the investment property calculator.

Many first-time property investors enter the field of real estate investing with a desire to start generating money and creating wealth. However, many of them fail even before they purchase the first investment property. Why? There are different reasons for this. But the main reason is the ever-changing state of the real estate market.

The real estate investing business keeps changing daily and is not the same as it was years ago. What might have been a great location or a great investment strategy might now be a bad one. Thanks to the improved technologies, now property investors can access different real estate investing tools to allow them to make successful real estate decisions. One of those tools is the investment property calculator.

This section will explore the investment property calculator. You will learn its uses, and why every motivated real estate investor has to join the class of successful property investors. Without further ado, let us jump right in!

Investment property calculator

This is a real estate investing tool that successful real estate investors use to calculate and attain projections for an investment property to find out its rate of return on investment. Therefore, using this online tool, property investors key in the necessary information about an income property and the investment property calculator will then show all the important figures required to indicate whether or not to purchase this income property.

If you don't know where you can find this fantastic

tool, Mashvisor is a real estate website that provides investors with an investment property calculator that uses predictive and traditional analytics. Still, you can research online to find other powerful investment property calculator tools.

What does the investment property calculator calculate?

As said before, property investors use this versatile tool to find projections and calculations related to the rental property and return on investment. Well, what are these exactly?

Cash on cash return

The cash on cash return is the net operating income (NOI) over the total cash investment. Computing cash on cash return allows property investors to see the expected return on investment they'd make if they pay for purchasing the rental property all in stock vs. with mortgage. When it comes in the real estate investment business, investment properties with a cash on cash return of about 8% are excellent investments.

Cap rate

The cap rate refers to the return on investment a real estate investor attains when computing the NOI and dividing it by the income property's value. For instance, if the NOI of an income property is $10, 000, and its value is $100, 000, the cap rate is 10%. Property investors are encouraged to invest in an income property that has a cap rate of 10% or even more.

Cash flow

Cash flow is the difference between monthly rental income and monthly costs of an income property. It comes in the form of the monthly rent collected from tenants, and it can be positive or negative. As a real estate investor, you always want to invest in a positive cash flow investment property. Negative cash flow means the expenses surpass the profits, which results in losing money from your rental property.

Why you need an investment property calculator

Successful real estate investors use this tool to make smart investment decisions efficiently. A real estate investor can use the investment property calculator to:

Analyze investment properties

Analyzing an income property is an excellent step before making the purchase. A real estate investor has to ensure that his/her investment will generate profit he/she is looking for. As such, an essential aspect for a successful real estate investing career is to purchase the right rental property.

Determine the optimal rental strategy

Another feature for successful real estate investing is finding out the optimal rental strategy. As a real estate investor, you can lease out your property as a long-term traditional rental. This decision is based on different factors, and it'll affect the return of an income property. That is why you need to be careful when making this investment decision. Fortunately, the investment property calculator can help you out!

To sum up

The secret to successful real estate investing lies in making smart investment decisions. So, whether you are a beginner real estate investor wanting to purchase your first investment property, or an experienced real estate investor searching for your next rental property, be smart and make use of the investment property calculator.

More secrets of successful real estate investors

Location, location, location

This point cannot be stressed anymore. Regardless of whether you are a beginner or a seasoned investor, the area is a critical factor that determines your probability of success.

Where you choose to invest in real estate has two different meanings. First, it means which city you decide to invest in. Also, it means which property you choose to invest in.

For instance, you may realize that although you live

in California, you might not be able to invest in its real estate market. You might decide to invest in the Texas real estate market, which is more profitable and affordable for you. On the other side, the exact location of the property in Texas is important.

Understand the rules and regulations

If you are just getting started in real estate investing, then the first rule is to understand the laws. There is no point in purchasing an investment property that you cannot take advantage of. Buying an investment property that you cannot use is a big waste of time and money. To avoid losing money, ensure that you read the rules and regulations specific to the city you are interested in before you purchase.

Finally, take your time when selecting a new investment strategy. Making money from your first rental property can have you on your way to a fruitful real estate investing career.

Conclusion

Real estate investing can be a challenging industry to enter, but mastering the various options present can help new investors to get a better understanding of how to make money. Investing in real estate will only continue to expand as the value of properties increase in cities across the United States.

The kind of real estate investing displayed on a TV or hear from professionals is not the only type of real estate investing.

There are different methods to generate money in real estate. Some of these methods may require more than 40 hours per week, while some may need only 40 hours per year. The time you spend to grow your real estate business depends on your personality, skills, knowledge, and timeline.

Probably you have heard this age-old question, "if you suddenly won one million dollars, and didn't have to work anymore, what would you have done?" The answer to this question, some say, reveals the career field you enter.

Remember, you don't need to make real estate investing your career in building wealth. If you love your current job, you don't need to quit it. Still, you can attain similar results by investing on the side.

www.ingramcontent.com/pod-product-compliance
Lightning Source LLC
Chambersburg PA
CBHW070635220526
45466CB00001B/180